IMAGES OF WAR

THE ITALIAN CAMPAIGN 1943–1945

This book is dedicated to Paul Burnett,
with thanks for his technical assistance during its preparation.

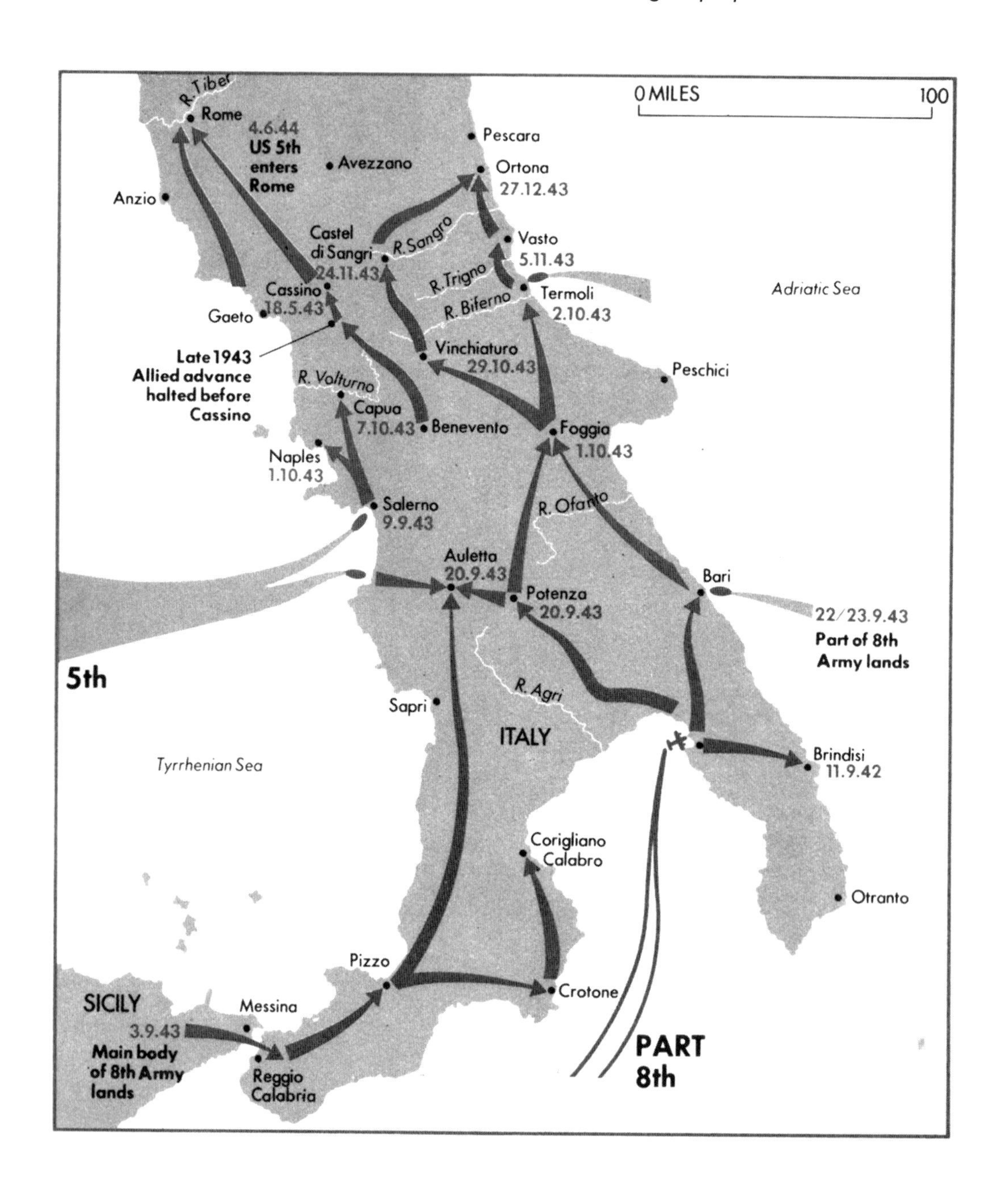

IMAGES OF WAR

THE ITALIAN CAMPAIGN 1943–1945

RARE PHOTOGRAPHS FROM WARTIME ARCHIVES

PHILIP JOWETT

Pen & Sword
MILITARY

First published in Great Britain in 2023 by
PEN & SWORD MILITARY
An imprint of
Pen & Sword Books Ltd
Yorkshire – Philadelphia

ISBN 978 1 39907 311 0

A CIP catalogue record for this book is available from the British Library.

Printed and bound in the UK by CPI Group (UK) Ltd, Croydon, CR0 4YY

Pen & Sword Books Limited incorporates the imprints of Atlas, Archaeology, Aviation, Discovery, Family History, Fiction, History, Maritime, Military, Military Classics, Politics, Select, Transport, True Crime, Air World, Frontline Publishing, Leo Cooper, Remember When, Seaforth Publishing, The Praetorian Press, Wharncliffe Local History, Wharncliffe Transport, Wharncliffe True Crime and White Owl.

For a complete list of Pen & Sword titles please contact

PEN & SWORD BOOKS LIMITED
47 Church Street, Barnsley, South Yorkshire, S70 2AS, England
E-mail: enquiries@pen-and-sword.co.uk
Website: www.pen-and-sword.co.uk

Or

PEN AND SWORD BOOKS
1950 Lawrence Rd, Havertown, PA 19083, USA
E-mail: Uspen-and-sword@casematepublishers.com
Website: www.penandswordbooks.com

Contents

German Defence Lines in Italy 1943–45

Albert Line – also known as the **Trasimene Line**, ran from the Ombrone River on the west coast to the east coast, north of Pescara. It was intended that this defence line would hold the Allies from June to July 1944, until the Gothic Line was ready.

Adige Line – extended east and west of Lake Garda. It was a substantial defence line with a trench system and was intended to cover the German withdrawal into Northeast Italy and Austria, spring 1945.

Autumn Mist Line – proposed as a defence line for the winter of 1944/45 but made redundant when Field Marshal Kesselring decided instead to defend river lines heading into the Po Valley.

Barbara Line – this temporary defence line started at the north of the Trigno River and ran south-west to the head of the Volturno River, October 1943.

Caesar Line – this defence line was built in the Alban Hills to the south of Rome, June 1944.

Gustav Line – the first substantial German defence line built across Italy halfway between Naples in the south and Rome in the centre of the country, January to May 1944.

Hitler Line – built in the mountains to the north of Cassino and was attacked in May 1944; when it looked like it was going to fall, it was renamed the **Senger Line**.

Venetian Line – ran along the Adige River to the south-west of Venice.

Viktor Line – also known as the Volturno Line, ran along the Volturno River in the west of Italy, then north of Naples to the Biferno River in the east. It was designed to hold the Allies until the larger Gustav Line was prepared in mid-October 1943.

Introduction

Italy 1943-45
The 'Soft Underbelly'

As the renowned military historian A.J.P.Taylor said, the Italian Campaign was 'born of compromise, continued in discord and ended in controversy'. It was the perfect example of the opposing concepts of war of the USA and Great Britain, which often frustrated the Allied war effort. In the USA's view, the direct assault from Great Britain into France was the obvious route to liberating occupied Europe. Their almost unlimited resources favoured this policy while Great Britain, with its resources stretched throughout the Empire, looked for other less 'costly' routes to liberation. Winston Churchill believed in 1943 that Italy, the now junior partner in the Axis alliance, was the weak link that could be exploited. Italy was the 'soft underbelly' of Axis Europe and Churchill, as he had with the Ottoman Empire in 1915, saw an opportunity to knock them out of the war. For the USA, Italy was always going to be a 'sideshow' to its war against Nazi Germany and against Imperial Japan. Although both Allied powers were to fight side by side in Italy from July 1943 until May 1945, their co-operation was often difficult, with regular disagreements over strategy. Hitler was torn between propping up his ally Mussolini or abandoning him to Allied attacks and pulling up the drawbridge. He was to waste hundreds of thousands of his troops defending Italy that could have been utilised more usefully in defending Northwest Europe and on the Eastern Front.

After two and a half years of fighting in North Africa from December 1940 to May 1943, the Allies had finally defeated the Afrika Korps and their Italian allies. The surrender of the remaining Axis forces in Tunisia in May 1943 meant that the 'battle-hardened' 8th Army and US forces were now available to fight elsewhere. Discussions between Winston Churchill and US President Roosevelt and their military commanders chose Sicily, the Italian island close to North Africa, as their first objective. Mussolini's Italy was in crisis and the main aim of an attack on Italian territory was to undermine the Fascist leader's power. Hitler's decision to fight for Italy meant that the military 'sideshow' that was the Italian Campaign was to prove a very costly one for both Axis and Allied forces. The arduous campaign fought over mountains and valleys saw the Germans and their Italian Fascist allies fight for every inch of the country. In effect, the twenty-four-month campaign was a fighting withdrawal by the German Army up the Italian peninsula. Well-prepared German defence lines saw the Allied armies often held up for months in battles that resulted in horrendous losses on both sides. Fighting at places like Anzio, Cassino and along the Gustav and Gothic lines saw some of the fiercest battles of the Second World War. Both sides tied up hundreds of thousands of troops in a bitterly fought campaign that in the end did not substantially affect the result of the greater world conflict.

By April 1945, the campaign involved a total of 1,333,856 Allied troops and support personnel and a staggering 4,000 aircraft. By the same date, there were 439,000 German troops fighting in Italy as well as 160,000 Italians who had remained loyal to their Axis partners. By that time, the Luftwaffe presence in Italy, which had stood at 700 planes in September 1943, had been reduced to only seventy-nine aircraft as the German defences finally cracked. If anyone has any doubt about the bitterness of the fighting in Italy, you only need to look at the casualty figures for the campaign. In the fighting on the Italian mainland from September 1943 to May 1945, the USA lost 29,560 dead and 82,180 wounded, while the British lost a total of 89,440 dead and wounded. Other Allied deaths included 4,720 Indians, 5,400 Canadians, 2,100 New Zealanders, 2,460 Poles, 710 South Africans, 8,660 Free French and 510 Brazilians. Losses on the German side were at a conservative estimate of 59,940 dead and 163,600 wounded, with their Italian Fascist allies losing 35,000 dead. The shelling and bombing of towns and cities of Italy led to a high death rate amongst the civilian population, with an estimated 153,000 dead.

Chapter One

Sicily 1943 Build-up to Invasion

Once the Axis forces in North Africa had been effectively defeated in spring 1943, there was much discussion between the Allied powers regarding the question, what next? The USA had no appetite for suggestions by Churchill regarding a possible invasion of Italy. They were, however, willing to discuss potential objectives in the Mediterranean that would clear the sea routes in the region. The USA favoured an invasion of the Italian island of Sardinia and the liberation of the French island of Corsica. To the British, the obvious objective for an invasion was the island of Sicily, which was only a short distance across the Strait of Messina to mainland Italy. Sicily was situated to the south-west of the Italian mainland and was only a short distance from Tunisia to the south-west and southern Italy to the north-east. In the sea off southern Sicily were a group of small Italian islands that dominated the channel between the island and North Africa. There were strong garrisons on the two main islands, Pantelleria and Lampedusa, which were fortified with concrete gun emplacements. Other smaller islands, Lampione and Linosa, also had small garrisons but were not expected to defend themselves. Pantelleria, known in Italy as 'the Italian Gibraltar', is surrounded by cliffs, and with its 12,000-strong garrison was expected to put up a strong fight against the Allied invaders. Some of its garrison had been evacuated from Tunisia when it fell to the Allies in May and may not have been expected to put up much of a fight due to war-weariness. Pantelleria had a mobile reserve of five battalions, largely made up of the well-disciplined Finance Guard. They had been transferred from the Austrian–Italian border and were regarded as second-line but well-trained troops. Lampedusa had a 4,000-strong garrison but there was no natural water supply for them and Mussolini did not expect them to fight. The Allied invasion of Pantelleria, Operation Corkscrew, began on 11 June, led by 14,000 British troops. These included British Commandos and the 1st Battalion of the Duke of Wellington's Regiment. Neighbouring islands Lampedusa and Linosa fell on 12 and 13 June, clearing the way for the projected invasion of Sicily. The Italian dictator had pragmatically given the islands' garrisons permission to surrender if the Allies decided to land on them. There were now few illusions as to where the Allied were to go next, and the Axis garrison of Sicily waited for the inevitable invasion.

The Italian dictator Benito Mussolini is seen at the height of his powers in 1938, when he was the peace broker of the Munich Agreement between Nazi Germany and Great Britain and France. Mussolini's popularity waned during the conflict as the Italian population began to suffer from the privations of war. Even as the invasion of Sicily began, many Italians still had deep loyalty to him and his Fascist regime. It was up to his own inner circle to vote him from power during a meeting of the Fascist Grand Council. The majority of the population then showed their true feeling as images and statues of him were torn down all over Italy. (*Author's Collection*)

Below: Anti-aircraft crews of the Fascist MVSN (Voluntary Militia for National Security) in Sicily prepare their shells for their Cannone da 76/40 76mm guns, which are out of date, like much of the Italian weaponry in 1943. They wear the M16 Adrian steel helmet, which had been worn by the Italian Army until the mid-1930s. These men are second-class troops who were either unfit or too old for first-line service and had to perform other civil defence roles. (*Author's Collection*)

A battery of Cannone da 76/40 76mm anti-aircraft guns are firing at Allied bombers from their emplacements in Sicily. By 1940, when Italy entered the war on Germany's side, this gun was outdated but had to remain in service until 1945. Its crew are from the MVSN anti-aircraft Militia and wear obsolete model M16 steel helmets and cast-off army shirts and breeches. *(Author's Collection)*

In the build-up to the invasion of Sicily, a tank unit takes part in an exercise with their obsolete FIAT 3000B light tanks. This tank is an improved version of the original 1920 model, which was only armed with twin Fiat machine guns. The tank is armed with a 37mm gun, which was a great improvement on the previous armament but still totally outdated by 1943. *(Author's Collection)*

In 1941, the Germans handed a number of ex-French R35 and S35 tanks to the Italian Army. The Italians did not use them in the front line despite the shortage of good tanks in their armoured divisions. Many found their way to Sicily, where they were formed into a new armoured formation, the 101st Tank Battalion. (*Author's Collection*)

The five-man crew of an Italian Semovente da 90/53 pose with their self-propelled gun on Sicily. Out of only thirty examples of this effective weapon that were built, twenty-four were stationed in Sicily in 1943. They were concentrated in the 10th Raggruppamento Semoventi and saw action during the Allied invasion. A few surviving 90/53s were seized by the Germans at the end of the fighting but proved to be useless in mountainous northern Italy where they were sent. (*Author's Collection*)

The crew of a coastal battery prepare to get their 152/50 152mm gun into action in the build-up to the invasion of Sicily. There were forty coastal batteries around the Sicilian coastline and the guns in them ranged from 76mm field guns to 381mm heavy guns. Batteries were manned largely by Fascist Blackshirt Militia and Coastal Artillery Groups, which were part of the Coastal Division structure. There were also a number of Motorised Artillery Groups equipped with guns from 75mm to 149mm. (*Author's Collection*)

A German quad 2cm Flakvierling 38 anti-aircraft gun crew in Sicily in the summer of 1943 scan the skies for any potential invaders. After the 8th Army's victory in North Africa, the Axis powers knew that Italy was the most likely objective for the Allies to strike at next. Intelligence reports were issued by the Allies to try to convince the Germans that Greece, Corsica or Sardinia were other feasible invasion objectives. (*Author's Collection*)

This patrol of British troops has taken one of the Italian gun positions on the island of Pantelleria on 11 June 1943. The island was well defended by a system of well-entrenched pillboxes and twenty-one gun batteries of various calibres. There were also 100 emplacements, some of which were concrete and others built into the cliff sides and mountains. They have captured the position of a Cannone da 76/40 anti-aircraft gun, which was a modernisation of a 3-inch Vickers. (*Author's Collection*)

Three British troops scramble over an Italian fuel dump on the island of Pantelleria during Operation Corkscrew. They belong to the 1st Battalion, Duke of Wellington's Regiment, a unit whose troops were mainly enlisted in West Yorkshire. The soldier at the front of the group is Lance Sergeant A. Haywood from Sheffield, who had won the Military Medal during the Tunisian Campaign. *(Author's Collection)*

Admiral Gino Pavesi, the commander-in-chief of the 12,000-strong garrison of the island of Pantelleria, is seen after being captured during its fall. The attack on the strategic island was costly for the RAF, with fifteen aircraft being shot down by Pantelleria's anti-aircraft defences. Ground fighting for the island was short-lived but resulted in forty dead and 150 wounded on the Italian side. (*Author's Collection*)

In the aftermath of the fall of Pantelleria, a British Army bulldozer clears away rubble of the bombing in the dock area. The heavy bombing of the island was seen as a test case for the proposed bombing of targets on Sicily and then on the Italian mainland. At this stage of the war, the Allies were still developing tactics that were to become the norm in the fighting of 1943–45. (*Author's Collection*)

Chapter Two

'Operation Husky' 1943 The Sicilian Campaign

After the fall of Pantelleria and the other small islands in early June, the garrison of the island of Sicily was on high alert. During the last months of June, Allied bombing raids on Sicilian towns and military installations left the island's defenders under no illusions as to what was coming. The garrison of Sicily, under the command of Italian General Alfredo Guzzoni, was largely made up of the Italian 6th Army. In total, there were four regular Italian divisions along with six Coastal divisions, which were made up of 'poor-quality' second-line troops. There were also two German infantry divisions and one armoured division, the 'Hermann Göring' Panzer Division, which had ninety-nine tanks in two battalions and three infantry battalions. The 15th Panzergrenadier Division had three Panzergrenadier regiments and a Tank battalion with sixty tanks.

Operation Husky, the Allied invasion of Sicily, began at dawn on 10 July 1943 when 160,000 men and 600 tanks landed on the island's southern and eastern coasts. The invasion was launched in bad weather, with heavy losses amongst the Allied landing ships, including 200 put out of action. General Alexander's 15th Army Group – US 7th Army under General Patton and the British 8th Army under General Montgomery – landed at two sectors: 7th Army landed on the southern coast at Gela, Licata and Scoglitti, where they faced the Italian 207th Coastal Division and 18th Coastal Brigade. On the 11th, the German and Italian forces counter-attacked towards US forces at Gela, with the 'Hermann Göring' Armoured Division and the Livorno Infantry Division attacking. 8th Army landings at several points of the south-east coast met little resistance and they advanced inland. 8th Army troops took Augusta on the 13th while Patton's 7th Army was still coming under heavy German-Italian counter-attacks. Once the Axis attacks had been blunted, the 7th Army went over to the offensive from the 14th, with I Corps heading westwards and another advancing northwards. The 8th Army took the town of Caltagirone on the 16th but was countered by growing German opposition to the south of Catania. 7th Army's two corps continued their two-pronged offensives and took Porto Empedocle on 17 July and Caltanissetta on the 18th. Montgomery and his 8th Army began to advance into the centre of the island on the 19th, with Agira and Enna being taken on the 20th.

Meanwhile, Patton's 7th Army advanced to the north-west and north-east on two axes, with Corleone falling on the 21st and Palermo on the 22nd. The westerly advance of the US forces saw the port of Trapani fall on the 22nd, and in the north, Termini fell the following day. On the 24th, Cefalù on the northern coast fell to the 7th Army, but German resistance remained firm in the centre of the island where a thrust towards Nicosia was held on the 27th. At the same time, an 8th Army advance against Agira in the centre of the island stalled, making little progress by the 27th. Both Agira and Nicosia fell on the 28th and the fighting now focused on the north-east of Sicily, where the majority of German forces were positioned. Troina, held by a German-Italian garrison, was surrounded by US troops and held out against the 7th Army until 6 August. Other Allied advances by the 8th Army were still held south of Catania and Mount Etna. On the northern coast, Sant'Agata did not fall until 8 August.

Over the next week, the German-Italian units began a steady withdrawal to the north-east of the island and the port of Messina. The 8th Army now pushed towards the port but came under heavy fire in the country to the south and east of Mount Etna. By 12 August, the US 7th Army was also advancing rapidly eastwards to stop the evacuation of Axis troops from Messina. Rearguard actions by some German and Italian units that were still fighting allowed their comrades to be transported across the Strait of Messina to mainland Italy. By 16 August, the 7th Army was moving into the outskirts of the port of Messina and it was now time to evacuate as many Axis troops as possible. On 17 August, American troops entered Messina in the north-east of Sicily a few hours ahead of the British. The last ten days of fighting had been extremely slow and bitter, and the satisfaction of having liberated Sicily was tempered by the fact that 40,000 German and 62,000 Italian troops had succeeded in evacuating across the Strait of Messina. They had taken with them fifty tanks and 100 field guns, which could now be used to defend southern Italy. Allied air and naval forces were unable to interdict this evacuation while senior commanders gave little thought to mounting an immediate pursuit into mainland Italy. While the early stages of the campaign were underway, the Italian dictator Benito Mussolini was being overthrown by his Grand Council on 24 July. In his meeting with the Italian King Victor Emmanuel III the following day, his long support for the monarchy made no difference and Mussolini was put under house arrest. During the Sicilian Campaign, both sides suffered heavy losses, with 4,678 Italians killed and 32,500 wounded, while German losses were 4,325 killed and 13,500 wounded. On the Allied side, 8th Army losses were 2,938 dead and 9,212 wounded, while US 7th Army losses were 2,811 killed and 6,471 wounded.

On the morning of 9 July 1943, British troops ride ashore on Sicily from their landing craft aboard a Universal Carrier (Bren Gun Carrier). The 8th Army landed on the eastern coast of the island with the 5th and 50th divisions coming ashore south of Syracuse. 30 Corps landed around Cape Passaro with 1st Canadian Division and 51st Highland Division, along with the 31st Brigade. (*Author's Collection*)

On 10 July, the first day of the Allied landings on Sicily, an American soldier drags a mule ashore from a landing craft with landing ships in the background. In anticipation of the difficult terrain that they would face, the US Army had purchased a number of mules in Tunisia. These animals were to prove vital during the coming fighting both in Sicily and on the Italian mainland. (*US Army Archives*)

Demoralised and dishevelled, Italian soldiers of the 206th Coastal Division are seen after their capture during the early stages of the Allied invasion of Sicily. The Coastal troops were given little training and were issued with old uniforms dating from the early 1930s. These included the M1916 steel helmet, which had been issued to the Italian Army during the First World War. (*Author's Collection*)

Happy looking Italian soldiers wave their white flags as they walk into captivity past the news cameraman. When the Allied invasion began, the 'poor quality' of most troops in the Sicily garrison became apparent. Many of these men in the Coastal divisions of the Italian Army had been seen as unfit for first-line duty. However, when the Allies invaded the Italian mainland, they came up against some elite formations made up of hard-line Fascists that were willing to fight to the death. (*Author's Collection*)

A mixed unit of German and Italian Coastal troops move a 20mm Flak 18 to a new position during the battle for Sicily. Although many Italian troops surrendered to the invading Allies, some units situated close to German formations had little choice but to fight. The Germans and Italians had always had a troubled relationship, especially in the Western Desert, where the Afrika Korps saw some of Mussolini's troops as a nuisance. *(Author's Collection)*

This ex-French R35 of the 3rd Platoon, 2nd Company, 101st Tank Battalion has been disabled by an American M4 Sherman tank in Gela. Most Italian tanks defending Sicily were either 1920s era Fiat 3000 light tanks or R35s handed over to them by the Germans. With the best Italian equipment and weaponry lost in North Africa and on the Eastern Front, the defenders of Sicily were left with the unwanted and obsolete in 1943. *(Author's Collection)*

This US Army 105mm field howitzer is firing towards German lines on Sicily on 14 August 1943. The 7th Army by this date was approaching the city of Messina, and took it on the night of the 16th/17th. In this probably staged scene, one crewman gets a shell out of the shell case and hands it to another crewman, who carries it over his shoulder or cradles it to the gun. *(Author's Collection)*

US Army Engineers use a SCR 625 mine detector to try to locate mines laid by the Germans at a river crossing in Sicily. This mine detector was the main model used by the US Army during the Second World War and operated with a metal coil attached to a searching rod. The operator had a satchel that carried the batteries for the device and he wore a pair of headphones that indicated when a mine was in the vicinity. In Sicily, the German Army was well trained in defence measures and the Allies were to come up against constant obstacles to their advance. (*US Army Archives*)

From the shelter of a stone wall that is being used as an observation post, US troops observe and monitor the effect of their artillery fire on a Sicilian town. The officer sitting down on the right is in communication by telephone with his unit's command post. In the centre of the group, one of his men uses a battery commander's telescope, or BC scope, while the other man uses binoculars. The Americans had learned some hard lessons during the Tunisian Campaign, including about the quality of the equipment they used. New optical equipment was part of the upgrade of all US military equipment, which was to serve them well during the coming two years of war. *(US Army Archives)*

A German Artillery observer from the Hermann Göring Division looks out from his hilltop position in central Sicily in the general direction that the advancing Allied armies were expected to come from. The Allied advance through the island was under constant pressure from artillery positions like this and from well-organised counter-offensives. (*Author's Collection*)

A heavy field gun position of the German Army in central Sicily fires at the advancing Allied troops. The loader of the 15cm schwere Feldhaubitze sFH 18 gun throws a spent shell case onto a pile behind him. This gun was the mainstay of the German Army's heavy field artillery and was supplied to allies like Italy and Finland. (*Author's Collection*)

This wire photograph with its clarity affected by static interference shows an Italian OM Autocarretta 36P light truck with two of its crew lying dead on the road. Italian troops continued to fight during the defence of Sicily with two divisions, the Aosta and Napoli, which were mainly made up of Sicilians. The population of Sicily was notoriously anti-Mussolini and the loyalty of the two divisions must have been suspect. (*Author's Collection*)

General Montgomery, the commander of the 8th Army, is seen aboard a DUKW amphibious carrier touring around the Sicilian towns already taken by his troops in the early fighting. The fact that Montgomery is standing up as he moves through the town centre implies that there was no threat of sniper fire from German troops. (*Author's Collection*)

In a break from the fighting for a Sicilian town, a US Army photographer has cleverly posed a soldier in front of an Italian First World War memorial. He sits at the foot of the memorial with his M2 carbine and has a quick nap before going back to his frontline unit. The soldier is Sergeant Norwood Dorman of Benson, North Carolina, who has just completed an arduous march from Brolo. (*Author's Collection*)

This lamp post in the centre of Messina aptly shows several features of the campaign in Sicily. Nailed to the post is a 1930s portrait of Benito Mussolini in all his Fascist finery; it has been vandalised by civilians who did not support the Italian dictator. The Sicilian population was renowned for their hatred of Mussolini and his regime, and many welcomed the Allied invasion. Also nailed to the post is a German military sign that points to the local 'Translation Agency'. (*Author's Collection*)

Another of the early victories by the 8th Army was the capture of Noto, through which these soldiers are marching on their way to Syracuse. The seaport of Syracuse was connected by a railway running from Pachino and was captured on 11 July. These men belong to the 2nd Battalion of the Seaforth Highlanders, which had fought at El Alamein in Egypt and in Tunisia before landing in Sicily. (*Author's Collection*)

General Matthew Ridgway poses on a road with his staff near the port of Ribera in south-western Sicily on 25 July. In April 1943, Ridgway's 82nd Airborne Division had been sent to North Africa in preparation to take part in the invasion of Sicily. The general complained that his troops had only received a fraction of the training given to other US divisions. Confusion during the airborne assault on Sicily meant that out of the 5,300 men of his division, Ridgway ended up with only 400 under his direct command during the early days of the campaign. (*US Army Archives*)

A German Panzergrenadier is about to go into action in Sicily and has covered his M35 helmet with foliage. He has been issued with an out-of-date MG15 light machine gun, which was not in common use with the Wehrmacht in 1943. The MG15 was originally designed as an aircraft gun but was converted for ground use by the addition of a bipod due to a high demand for machine guns. *(Author's Collection)*

This British paratrooper has fallen into German hands during the fighting for Sicily and is being interrogated by his captors. At least one of the men questioning him is a fellow paratrooper – Fallschirmjäger – who may or may not have empathy for his captive. During the Sicilian Campaign, there were two airborne operations by the British: Fustian, involving 1,856 men, and Ladbroke. The latter involved a glider assault that went terribly wrong, with 252 airborne troops drowning when their transports crashed into the sea. *(Author's Collection)*

German mechanics work on a StuG III Sturmgeschütz 40 Ausf. F/8 under the shade of a Sicilian olive tree. The anti-tank destroyer equipped the 1st Fallschirm-Panzer Hermann Göring Panzer Division during the campaign. Personnel for the Hermann Göring Division came largely from the ranks of ex-Hitler Youth and were all fanatical Nazis. (*Author's Collection*)

Two US Army medics of the 1st Infantry Division treat a wounded comrade during the fighting for Sicily. Their division belongs to the US 2nd Corps, which was made up of the 1st and 45th divisions. The 1st had fought in Tunisia while the 45th had arrived from the USA via the North African port of Oran. While the 45th was in Oran, the division had received training in amphibious warfare in preparation for the invasion of Sicily. *(Author's Collection)*

Like all armies throughout history, this US Army unit in Sicily have adapted what they found locally on the island to transport them. These donkey carts would save a great deal of shoe leather as they advance across the island to meet the German and Italian defenders. Hopefully, the confiscation of the donkeys and their carts from local farmers would have been compensated if the Americans wanted to win the islanders' 'hearts and minds'. *(Author's Collection)*

A US Army M7 Priest self-propelled gun moves through a Sicilian town as the Allied forces begin to gain supremacy over the German and Italian defenders. It was the sheer amount of weaponry such as this M7 that contributed to the Allied victory in Sicily, but the Axis forces fought for every village and town. (*US Army Archives*)

An American M3 GMC half-track motor gun carriage with a 75mm gun mounted in the back moves through a Sicilian town. The improvised self-propelled gun carrier was used in large numbers in Sicily but was soon to be replaced by the M10, a specifically designed tank destroyer. This M3 has a 75mm PACK howitzer fitted instead of the standard field gun and may have been improvised in theatre. (*US Army Archives*)

A French-Moroccan Goumier sharpens his M1905 bayonet for his US-supplied M1903 rifle during a break in the fighting for Sicily. Goumiers in the French Colonial Army were recruited from particular Moroccan tribes and were supposed to act as muleteers. In reality, these tough soldiers fought alongside the frontline troops and soon gained a reputation for their bravery. This man's razor-sharp bayonet would be used in hand-to-hand combat, at which these tribesmen excelled. (*Author's Collection*)

An American soldier leads his mule along a mountain pass with his Garand M1 rifle at the ready. The north and centre of Sicily were mountainous and mules were often the only type of transport that could get supplies to forward units. Thankfully for the Allied troops, the planning for the invasion of Sicily and Italy included the purchasing of mules for this purpose. (*US Army Archives*)

These British soldiers move warily through a Sicilian village on the road to Syracuse on the eastern coast of Sicily. The 8th Army announced the fall of the port on 12 July, when the locals are recorded to have met the Allies with flowers and V-signs. In the village square lie three Italian soldiers who were killed defending it as some of Mussolini's troops continued to resist the invasion. (*Author's Collection*)

British and Canadian troops meet in the centre of Caltagirone having advanced on the town from opposite directions. The town fell on 16 July as part of the Allied advance into western Sicily as the US Army advanced along the northern coast, taking the town of Porto Empedocle. Fighting on the island was now drawing to a close, even as more German reinforcements were arriving from the mainland. (*Author's Collection*)

A column of Scottish soldiers advance across Sicily wearing the minimum of uniform in the searing heat of the summer. They do, however, wear the traditional bonnet tam-o'-shanter' with the regiment's silver badge pinned on the left side. Passing the Scottish troops along the road is a line of Sicilian carts full of refugees returning to their homes after the fighting had ended in their village or town. (*Author's Collection*)

At the end of the campaign in Sicily, a ship full of German officers still wearing their tropical uniforms has just arrived at a British port. As they walk past a welcoming party of British soldiers, the officers are handed food parcels from a trestle table. The defiance of some of the defeated Germans is shown by one of the officers, who seems to be distaining the food offered. In the original caption, the writer asks cheekily if the indignant officer 'wasn't hungry'. (*Author's Collection*)

Chapter Three

September–October 1943 Southern Italy

After the victory in Sicily, a plan for the invasion of the Italian mainland was debated by the Allied Command. Southern Italy and its proximity to Sicily and North Africa, where large numbers of Allied troops were still stationed, was the obvious site for any landings.

Once southern Italy was selected, it was decided to launch three separate invasion forces to land there. The first, Operation Avalanche, would involve the US 5th Army, which had been formed in January 1943 with troops sent from Oran, Bizerte and Libya in North Africa and from Palermo in Sicily. This first invasion force would land at the Italian port of Salerno in the south-west of the country. A second landing, Operation Baytown, would involve troops of the British 8th Army being transported the short distance across the Strait of Messina to the port of Reggio on the toe of Italy. The third invasion force of 8th Army troops would sail from Bizerte in Tunisia to the port of Taranto on the heel of the boot of Italy in Operation Slapstick. Ready to face the coming Allied landings were the German 10th Army with the 14th and the 76th Panzer corps. The 14th Panzer Corps, with 45,000 men, had the 15th and 16th Panzer divisions and the Hermann Göring Panzer Division. The 76th Panzer Corps, with 30,000 men, had the 26th Panzer Division, the 29th Panzergrenadier Division and the 1st Parachute Division, with 17,000 men. The 14th Panzer Corps were in position on the Tyrrhenian coast between Gaeta and Salerno, and the 76th Panzer Corps was in the toe of Italy opposite Messina. In the Foggia region was the strong 1st Parachute Division, with 17,000 men.

On 3 September, the first of the invasion forces, in Operation Baytown, General Montgomery's British XIII Corps landed at Reggio at 4.30 am. XIII Corps was made up of the British 5th Division and the 1st Canadian Division and their landing at Reggio was regarded by the Allies as a diversion to the coming US landings at Salerno, Operation Avalanche, in six days' time. The Royal Navy bombarded the port and when the British and Canadian troops first landed, they faced little resistance from the Axis forces. By the end of the day, Reggio, Catona, Melito and Bagnara had been taken by the troops who had already landed. The 5th Division moved up the peninsula on the left flank while the 1st Canadian advanced on the right flank. By 6 September, the 13th Corps advance had reached Palmi and Delianuova with little resistance, although constant German demolitions slowed their progress. By the 7th, XIII Corps had advanced into Calabria on the Nicastro–Catanzaro road towards the town of Pizzo. On the 8th, the 5th Division took Rosarno and Pizzo while the Canadians took the town of Catanzaro. From 8 to 13 September, the 8th Army paused while events in other regions of the south evolved. On 9 September, the US 5th Army under General Mark Clark landed at Salerno Bay in Operation Avalanche, which was further up the western Italian coast.

The 5th Army, with 170,000 troops, was made up of the US VI Corps and the British X Corps. Salerno is south of Naples and 150 miles from Rome and the landing there had effectively outflanked the German defenders in the south. Salerno was going to be a tough nut to crack, being surrounded by a ring of mountains, and German artillery took a heavy toll of the landing force. The 5th Army was pinned down by the Germans and there was talk of re-embarking the troops, but this was quashed by General Alexander. Field Marshal Kesselring, commanding the German Army, now ordered all units in southern Italy to fall back to contain the Salerno bridgehead. A German counter-attack began on the 11th, and on the 12th, the Hermann Göring Panzer Division drove the British from their positions at Molina Pass. At the same time, the Germans attempted to drive a wedge between the 8th Army and the newly landed 5th Army. The German offensive against the Salerno bridgehead was almost successful when they reached to within a mile of the beach. One of the German commanders, General Hube, had fought in Sicily and was determined not to repeat the defeat he had suffered there. To support the beachhead, reinforcements were landed and two battleships moored off the port, and their 15-inch guns battered the German positions. Heavy bombing by the USAF also began to affect the German defenders, who gradually withdrew from the vicinity of the beachhead.

While the fighting in southern Italy was underway, the political situation in the country was reaching a vital moment. The post-Mussolini Badoglio government was still outwardly loyal to its ally, Nazi Germany. Field Marshal Kesselring had been working in close co-operation with the Italian High Command, with plans to defend Italy. He believed the Italian head of state Marshal Badoglio's promises of loyalty to Germany and commitment to the Axis war effort. In contrast, Adolf Hitler had little or no trust in Badoglio and was positive that Italy would soon attempt to join the Allies. Secret negotiations between the Italians and the Allies had begun on 25 July 1943, with the full knowledge of the German secret services. On 8 September, the Italians surrendered to the Allies and immediately, German plans to take over Italy and Italian-occupied parts of Europe were put into action. Operation Achse saw sixty German divisions, including twenty-six in Italy since July, move to secure their control there as well as in the Balkans and southern France. Badoglio fled Rome and escaped south with his government as the Germany Army took the Italian capital. Any resistance by the Italian Army was swiftly dealt with by the Germans, whose behaviour on many occasions was brutal.

While there was a state of confusion in Italy, an Allied force landed in the south-east of the country, taking the port of Taranto, in Operation Slapstick. The British 1st Airborne Division took Taranto on 9 September and then moved swiftly on to take Brindisi on 11 September, and then Bari on the 14th. It was ironic that the main German force fighting the 1st Airborne were made up of units from the German 1st Parachute Division. As the political situation stabilised and the Germans took control of central and northern Italy, they launched a series of determined attacks from 13 to 15 September against the Allied bridgeheads in southern Italy. These were repulsed with help from RAF and USAF bombing and shelling from the Royal Navy off the coast. From the 13th, Montgomery's 8th Army continued its advance northwards and made contacts with infantry patrols of the 5th Army on 16 September and with the force that had landed at Taranto. Kesselring ordered the commander of the German 10th Army to begin withdrawing northwards towards the German defence line known as the Viktor Line. As the 10th Army withdrew steadily from the south, its engineers demolished roads and bridges in an attempt to slow down the Allies. The German commander of the 10th, General Vietinghoff, was told to hold this line until at least 15 October. This would give the engineers and workmen preparing the Gustav Line time to finish their work.

On 22 September, British reinforcements landed at Bari and a mixed group of 8th Army armoured and infantry pushed on to Foggia. The capture of Foggia on the 27th gave the Allied air forces possession of some important airfields, which were to be vital in the air war over Italy. On the 29th, General Alexander issued instructions to his commanders about future operations in Italy. He ordered an advance on the city of Naples followed by an advance to the Sessa Aurunca–Venafro–Isernia–Castropignano Line and the Biferno River. Alexander's first objective, Naples, was in sight, with the British X Corps breaking into the Naples Plain on the 26th. On the 28th, the X Corps resumed their advance towards Naples, and by the 30th, they had surrounded Mount Vesuvius, close to the city. In Naples, a mass rebellion by Italian resistance fighters and armed civilians broke out and liberated the city from the German occupiers. Naples was officially taken by advance units of the US 5th Army on 1 October. By the next day, the 8th Army had moved up to the Biferno River on the Adriatic coast and the US 5th Army was facing the Volturno River on the Tyrrhenian coast.

During the Allied landing at the port of Reggio, this Canadian signalman has received a head wound. After having his wound bandaged by a medic, the radio operator is carrying on in his vital role of keeping the various units in touch with each other. Two Canadian formations were part of the 8th Army's XIII Corps during the landings in southern Italy, the 1st Canadian Infantry Division and the 1st Canadian Artillery Brigade. (*Author's Collection*)

A column of DUKW amphibious trucks move through the port of Reggio manned by 8th Army soldiers. These 3-ton vehicles were manufactured in the USA and then sent as Lend-Lease to the British Army. The name of the vehicle was devised from four initials: D for model year 1942, U for the utility body style, K for all-wheel drive and W for dual wheel axles. These useful vehicles, generally called DUCKS by the soldiers, were in high demand by the Allied armies from 1942 until 1945. There was a constant shortage of DUKWs and the various theatre commanders vied to receive as many as they could for their formations. *(Author's Collection)*

German troops move a PAK38 anti-tank gun into position on the Italian coast in expectation of the Allied landings in southern Italy. After the conquest of Sicily, the Germans knew that the next objective for the British and US forces would be in south Italy. On 3 September, units of the XIII Corps of the British 8th Army landed at Reggio on the most southerly point of the Italian mainland. At first, resistance was light but it soon hardened as German and Italian units were sent to the landing points. *(Author's Collection)*

German troops move into northern Italy before moving southwards to try to counter the expected Allied landings on the mainland. This unit is made up of a German Sd Kfz 10/5 semi-track truck with a 20mm Flak 18 anti-aircraft gun mounted on its platform and an Italian Ansaldo AB41 armoured car. The armoured car, which served successfully with the Italians in North Africa from 1941, has been taken over by the Germans for their use. (*Author's Collection*)

A young German artillery spotter looks through his periscope in preparation for the next engagement with the Allied armies in southern Italy. Allied forces had landed at several locations in southern Italy in early September at Salerno, Calabria and Taranto. Allied hopes that the German Army in southern Italy would be isolated and surrounded by a hostile Italian population were not realised. (*Author's Collection*)

A 3-inch mortar of the 5th Battalion of the Hampshire Regiment fires towards German lines at Salerno. The landings in southern Italy were heavily challenged by German forces as they tried to stop the expansion of the initial Salerno bridgehead. Involved in the landings were the British X Corps and the US VI Corps of the 5th Army under the command of General Clark. *(Author's Collection)*

British troops have set up an observation post in an abandoned house during the fighting for the port of Salerno on 14 September. One man looks for likely targets through his binoculars while another man readies spare clips for the sub-machine-gunner. He is armed with the US-produced Thompson sub-machine gun, which was in widespread use alongside the Sten. *(Author's Collection)*

Panzer IV G medium tanks of the 16th Panzer Division are seen on the road to Salerno, where they will try to counter the recent Allied landings there. The 16th's commander, Major General Rudolf Sieckenius, had organised his tanks into four mixed battle groups, which were stationed 6 miles apart. It was the 'Dörnemann' Battle Group that was the first to make contact with British troops of the 46th Infantry Division, who had landed to the east of Salerno. *(Author's Collection)*

The crew of a British Army Bren Gun Carrier drive their personnel carrier through the narrow roads and lanes of the city of Salerno. Its crew crane their necks to see if their vehicle will fit down the road, which had been covered in rubble from the Allied bombardment. Tanks and other fighting vehicles often found the centre of cities, towns and villages in Italy difficult to traverse, with the worry that they might be attacked from the buildings they passed. *(Author's Collection)*

Right: A wounded British soldier belonging to the British Army's 10th Corps is carried to the advanced casualty station by two of his comrades during fighting around Salerno. During the fighting for Salerno, 982 British soldiers were killed and another 7,365 wounded. There were also a number of missing troops, most of whom returned to their units after the confusion of the fighting had died down. (*Author's Collection*)

Below: In the fighting around Salerno, a German MG42 machine-gun crew fire towards Allied positions. The continuing defence of Italy against the Allied armies was a major drain on German manpower. With almost 500,000 troops deployed in Italy, other more vital fronts were denuded of troops, tanks and artillery. This machine gun was one of the most potent weapons used by the Germans and captured examples were often put into service with the Allies or Italian partisans. (*Author's Collection*)

This 88mm anti-aircraft gun of the Italian Army undergoes a drill in anticipation of an Allied invasion of mainland Italy. A number of these German guns had been sold to Italy to increase the potency of their anti-aircraft defences. When the Italian officer commanding the coastal defences at Salerno hesitated in taking an order from a German major to open fire on the invaders, he was shot on the spot. (*Author's Collection*)

Panzergrenadiers of the 15th Division are pictured taking a break from the fighting for control of the Salerno bridgehead. They have been issued with Nazi propaganda magazines, which are full of the usual articles and photographs showing German victories. The 15th Panzergrenadier Division had seen service in Sicily and then at Salerno. Later it was to take part in the battles around Anzio and at Cassino. (*NAC*)

Above: Two German prisoners from the 16th Panzer Division opposing the landings at Salerno talk to two US officers, a Coastal Guardsman and an infantry officer. Casualties on the German side totalled 840 killed and 2,002 wounded, and the majority of these were sustained by the bombardment hitting the landing beaches from the Allied naval force supporting the invasion. (*US Army Archives*)

Right: This was the first photograph of Marshal Pietro Badoglio since the decision by his government to join the Allies. The 71-year-old was photographed at the Southern Headquarters of the Italian Royal Navy. He was Italian Prime Minister from 25 July 1943 until 8 June 1944, when he became Minister of Foreign Affairs. Badoglio had been an enthusiastic follower of Mussolini, even if only for career purposes, and conquered Ethiopia in 1936. Having resigned from his position as Chief of Staff of the Italian Army in 1940, he gradually came to agree that Mussolini must be replaced. Badoglio plotted with the Italian King Victor Emmanuel and took over as leader when the Italian dictator fell on 24 July 1943. (*Author's Collection*)

Above: German Panzer V Tiger heavy tanks pause on their journey into northern Italy from Germany along the Brenner Pass in early September 1943. The decision by Marshal Badoglio's government to join the Allies was met with a decisive and brutal German reaction. Troops and equipment were rushed into Italy to reinforce the already strong German forces stationed in the country. Officially, the German divisions in Italy were stationed there to protect their Italian allies, although everyone knew the real purpose for their presence. (*Cody Images*)

Left: A Panzerkampfwagen III medium tank is seen on the streets of an Italian city during the German takeover of the country in October 1943. Even before Mussolini fell from power on 25 July 1943, Hitler had been making plans to seize power in Italy. The anti-German attitude of the new Badoglio government soon became apparent and on 8 September, Operation Achse was launched. It took eleven days for the Germans to fully take control of Italy, which also involved the capturing of over 1 million Italian soldiers. (*Cody Images*)

A Luftwaffe 20mm Flakvierling 38 quad anti-aircraft gun is set up by its crew in the centre of Rome during Operation Achse. During the takeover of Italy by the German Armed Forces, all available forces already in the country were brought into action. Italian resistance to the German conquest of the country was in many cases fierce but short-lived. Hitler had ordered that any attempts by the Italian Armed Forces to resist his troops should be met with brutal measures. *(Author's Collection)*

Italian artillerymen prepare to fire their medium field gun at approaching German units trying to occupy Rome on 9 September. In the confused situation faced by the Italian surrender, some units were willing to fight their former allies. The poorly organised 20,000 defenders of Rome included units from the Ariete and Piave divisions and the Sardinian Grenadiers. Other smaller units that came forward to fight the Germans were made up of Carabinieri and a battalion of paratroopers. They were also joined by enraged civilians, who grabbed spare rifles and prepared to defend their city. Official Italian losses during the unsuccessful defence of Rome were 414 soldiers, and 183 civilians including twenty-seven women. *(Author's Collection)*

Right: Two German paratroopers stand guard over St Peter's Square next to the Vatican in the centre of Rome. When the Italian Government changed sides, the German Armed Forces in Italy put into action its well-planned reaction. These paratroopers look fairly relaxed, but Italian resistance to the German takeover did occur in some parts of the capital. The Italians were usually overawed by the efficiency and brutality of their former allies, who threatened any units that did not lay down their arms. (*Author's Collection*)

Below: The crew of a motorcycle and sidecar of the German 2nd Parachute Division stop and have a chat with comrades guarding St Peter's Square. During the German takeover of Italy there was some confusion on the German side, especially after an RAF bombing raid on Field Marshal Kesselring's headquarters at Frascati. The German commander threatened the Italians with a 700-bomber raid if they did not surrender. In reality, Kesselring only had 142 planes available in September 1943, but the bluff worked. (*Author's Collection*)

A German officer orders his men to move forward during the early stages of the defence of southern Italy. The German Army was facing landings at several points in the boot of Italy in the aftermath of the fall of Sicily. Fighting in the south saw the beginning of a long and costly campaign by the US 5th and British 8th armies to push the Germans up the Italian peninsula from September 1943 to May 1945. *(Author's Collection)*

The crew of a PAK 40 anti-tank gun have sited their weapon to control the main road into a town in southern Italy in September 1943. There were approximately 100,000 German troops stationed in the south of Italy when the Allied invasions began. These men are preparing to defend their position from the troops who had landed at the port of Salerno. Some of these troops had been transported across the Strait of Messina at the end of the Sicilian Campaign and were soon in combat again on the mainland. *(Author's Collection)*

The crew of a Sturmgeschütz III in southern Italy load their tank destroyer with shells brought to them by a supply truck. It was reported that the StuG III was very popular with its crews and its low profile made it a hard target for Allied tanks. They did have problems with the mechanical reliability of the StuG, which was prone to throw its tracks. This was due to a problem with the final drive units, which caused the tracks to come off in combat. (*NAC*)

This Flakvierling 38 Quad 20mm anti-aircraft gun of the German Army has been set up in the mountains of southern Italy during the fighting of late summer 1943. According to the original caption, the gun has been sited to protect the 'serpentine mountain roads along which supplies were sent to German units in some sectors of the southern Italian Front'. (*Author's Collection*)

A unit of German Sturmgeschütz III Ausf. G assault guns drive through Naples in preparation to resist the advance of Allied forces coming from the south of Italy. Based on the chassis of the PzKpfw III and armed with a 75mm Stuk 40 main gun, it was produced from late 1942. They were originally in eighteen vehicle assault gun battalions divided into three Batteries of six vehicles. Later it was decided to organise the assault guns into forty-five-strong brigades, with three batteries of fourteen and three HQ vehicles. (*NAC*)

An M4 Sherman medium tank moves cautiously through a town near Naples carrying infantry who are on the lookout for German snipers in the last days of September 1943. The small town is Torre Annunziata, which as the street sign suggests was close to the volcano Mount Vesuvius. During the Italian Campaign, German troops usually pulled back from a town when it fell in order to set up new defence lines. (*Author's Collection*)

In what became known as the *'Quattro giornate de Napoli'* – or 'Four Days of Naples' – the population of the city rose up to overthrow the German occupation. From 28 to 30 September, 1,500 armed Italians and thousands of supporters virtually liberated Naples from the Germans. They stopped the planned deportation of civilians arrested by the German occupiers and took arms from local depots. The popular rising forced the Germans to move out of the city as the 8th Army moved into the suburbs, liberating it for the second time on 1 October. *(Author's Collection)*

A Canadian infantryman moves cautiously along a street in Campochiaro to the north-east of Naples with a grenade ready to throw into a doorway. He and his comrades are trying to pin down a German machine-gun nest further down the street in typical street fighting. Heavy German resistance to the Allied advance meant that the conquest of Italy was going to take a long time. *(Author's Collection)*

US troops man a captured 2cm Flakvierling 38 quad anti-aircraft gun, which is mounted on a railway truck near Naples. Even though the US Army was well equipped, they would still utilise captured enemy weaponry, as all armies did during the Second World War. *(Author's Collection)*

A few hours after the entrance of the 5th Army into Naples, their commander, General Mark Clark, strolls around its streets. The Americans entered Naples at 9.45 am and his entourage included a mixture of US Army and British Army officers. When asked about the progress of the war, General Clark said that he was 'quite satisfied' with the situation in Italy. *(Author's Collection)*

Chapter Four

October–December 1943 Moving North

After consolidating their positions in southern Italy during September 1943, the Allies were ready by the beginning of October to push northwards towards the Gustav Line. Established in October 1943, the Gustav Line was still in the early stages of construction. It was to be the first of a number of major Axis defence lines that were intended to stop or at least slow the northwards advance of the Allied armies in Italy. The line was to follow the line of the rivers Garigliano and Rapido and was centred on the natural fortification provided by Monte Cassino, the monastery overlooking the town of Cassino. Further east, the Gustav Line turned northwards, ending on the Adriatic coast, south of the town of San Vito. Defending the Gustav Line were the 10th Army with General Hube's 14th Armoured Corps to the south and General Traugott Herr's 71st Armoured Corps to the north. Attached to the main defensive line were two shorter lines, which ran from the Tyrrhenian Sea to the vicinity of the town of Cassino. In order to reach the Gustav Line, the US 5th and British 8th armies would have to overcome a number of obstacles on their advance northwards. On the Adriatic coast, the 8th Army advance would have to cross three rivers, which were, from south to north, the Fortone, Biferno and Trigno. Meanwhile on the Tyrrhenian coast, the 5th Army was faced with crossing the Volturno River and the Liri River en route to its major objective, Rome. German forces were spread out all along the front and units would have to be moved around to face the two-pronged Allied offensive.

On 2 October, the British 3rd Commando landed at the port of Termoli on the north bank of the Biferno River. They seized the harbour and then joined with the British 78th Division, which was about to cross the Biferno. The 8th Army was then faced by the 16th Panzergrenadier Division, which had been switched from the Volturno River front. While fighting continued around Termoli, the 78th crossed the Biferno and forced the Germans to withdraw northwards to the Trigno River. By the 14th, the 78th had moved up to the Trigno and on the 22nd, they crossed the river and established a small bridgehead on the northern bank. It took almost two weeks to consolidate the bridgehead, which was achieved by 2 November. Once again, the Germans made an orderly withdrawal towards the Sangro River, which they crossed on the 19th. Some remnants of the German defenders remained on the opposite bank of the Sangro but were overwhelmed by the 8th Army offensive, which began on 28 November. The Allied advance reached the Moro River on the 6th and it was crossed between 8 and 10 December. Fighting around the Moro River was to last for a month, with the Allied victory over the Germans not coming until 4 January 1944. The defeated 76th Panzer Corps was trapped in the east and Kesselring was unable to move it to reinforce the Germans fighting the 5th Army. The 8th Army advance was again slowed but this time it was the terrible weather as well as the German resistance that held them up. Fighting around the towns of Orsogna and Ortona from 20 to 28 December saw strong German counter-attacks, which delayed the advance. It took until the 23rd for Orsogna to fall, and until the 28th when Ortona fell after vicious street fighting.

While the 8th Army were struggling up the Adriatic coast, the US 5th Army was moving up on the western coast of Italy. On 2 October, the 3rd Division of the US VI Corps was moving towards the Volturno River, while on the 4th, the 34th and 45th Infantry divisions were moving towards Benevento, an important rail junction. They took the junction and then crossed the Calore River and established a bridgehead on the opposite bank. In anticipation of the attack on the Volturno, the 16th Panzergrenadier Division had been replaced along the Volturno River by the 16th Armoured Division. On the 6th, the 5th Army reached the south bank of the Volturno River and the British 10th Division attached to the US 5th Army took the city of Capua, 25 miles to the north of Naples. The 5th Army took five days to prepare for its crossing of the Volturno, which began on the 12th. When the assault was launched across the river along a 40-mile front, it was badly affected by poor weather and strong German resistance. They were faced by tough German units of the 15th Armoured Division, Hermann Göring Armoured Division and 3rd Infantry Division, who slowed the 5th Army's advance. On the 13th, the US 3rd and 34th divisions succeeded in crossing the Volturno on the right of the front while the 45th Division took Monte Acero. On 5 November, the 5th Army launched a series of attacks to try to break through the Bernhardt Line. This line was the last defence that protected the Gustav Line from the Allied offensive. In the advance to the Bernhardt Line, a series of battles were fought for the German stronghold on Monte Camino. Ten days of battle in poor weather conditions were fought against the German 14th Armoured Corps by the British 56th Division, centred on Monte Camino. This position was contended over for a month, with new attacks beginning after a lull on 5 December and the German defences falling the next day. On the following day, the 5th Army began attacks against Monte Sammucro and San Pietro, with the mountain stronghold falling on the 17th, and the town the next day. In the aftermath of the December fighting, both the 5th and 8th armies moved tentatively towards the Gustav Line defences. It was to be mid-January 1944 before the Allies were in place to make the first of their assaults against the much-vaunted German defences.

An 8th Army BL 5.5-inch field gun fires towards German positions during the fighting in Italy in October 1943. As was common with most larger artillery pieces, this gun is protected by a large camouflage net. The 5.5-inch medium gun was first introduced into British Army service in 1941 and it played a vital role with the 8th Army in North Africa. *(Author's Collection)*

The South African Prime Minister Field Marshal Jan Smuts (centre) pays a visit to General Eisenhower and General Alexander in Italy in October 1943. Good relations and co-operation between the various Allies including South Africa were vital to the Allied war effort. The 73-year-old Smuts had fought against Britain during the 1899–1902 Boer War but had sided with his old enemies in 1914–18, and again from 1939. (*Author's Collection*)

German troops move a PAK 38 anti-tank gun down a mountain road during the fighting for southern Italy in October 1943. The men literally manhandle the gun, which weighed 2,341lb, and it will take all the strength of the eight-man crew to push and pull it into position. (*NAC*)

Above: The crew of a German Army 21cm Nebelwerfer 42 multi-barrelled rocket launcher prepare their weapon ready to fire at the Allied troops. These weapons were often organised into batteries of six launchers with three batteries per battalion. Larger formations of Nebelwerfers were made up of Werfer regiments and Werfer brigades. When properly deployed, the Nebelwerfer could be a devastating weapon, with similar weapons used by the other combatants. (*Author's Collection*)

Right: A gunner of an 88mm anti-aircraft weapon in southern Italy in 1943 cleans his gun's shells and then stacks them in their cases for future use. During the fighting in Italy, the difficult terrain often adversely affected the supply lines throughout the country. This meant that ammunition and other supplies had to be used sparingly and wastage was reduced to a minimum, especially on the German side. Afrika Korps cork sun helmets were still seen in use during the early fighting in Italy but were usually soon replaced by M35 steel helmets. (*NAC*)

The crew of a German heavy field gun prepare shells by fitting their fuses before stacking them for the gun loaders. Allied planners did not know how strong the German defence of southern Italy would be but Hitler had been persuaded to defend the south. This gun is part of the strong defensive measures taken by the Germans in southern Italy in the late summer of 1943. (*NAC*)

In the autumn of 1943, this 88mm anti-aircraft gun has its barrel raised to the maximum elevation ready to fire at Allied aircraft. The crewmembers are stripped to the waist in the searing heat of southern Italy while still wearing their M35 steel helmets. Wooden supports have been fitted to the top of the barrel, presumably to try to help absorb the recoil of the gun. (*NAC*)

German prisoners are brought across the Volturno River having been captured on the far bank during fighting there in mid-October. The British soldiers have decided to get their captives to do some of the work and have given them oars to use. Bridgeheads had been established over the other side of the river and these were contested by the German defenders. (*Author's Collection*)

The British crew of a 25-pounder field gun fire towards German positions along the banks of the Volturno River on 12 October. This gun is ready to give support to the US 5th Army, US 6th Corps and British 10th Corps preparing to cross the 300ft wide river. Although the river was wide, it was only 3ft deep along some sections and could be forded, but when the crossing took place, it was running high due to heavy rain. (*Author's Collection*)

This 2-inch mortar crew of the British Army are firing their gun from the ruins of Grazzanise, a town on the southern bank of the Volturno River, in early October. When the 5th Army crossed the river on 12–13 October, they faced heavy resistance from the German Army. The mortar was first introduced into British Army service in 1939 and was to give sterling service until 1945 and after. (*Author's Collection*)

British Engineers of the 5th Army are crossing the Volturno River near to Castello Volturno in October 1943. They belong to the 272 Field Company Royal Engineers and are carrying Universal Carriers of the 46th Infantry Division. These improvised river craft were formed by strapping wooden road sections to pontoon boats and then pulling them across the river like ferries. (*Author's Collection*)

A British Army Bren gunner and his comrade cover an advance along the Teano–Sessa Aurunca road in fighting close to the Teano River in late October 1943. They use the cover of a bank to try to protect them and the rifleman peers though a small bush. The British crossed the river on 29 October during their long and difficult march towards the Italian capital, Rome. (*Author's Collection*)

A unit of British Army armoured cars of the 5th Army move along a forest road towards a village called Roccamonfina. The village was north-east of Sessa Aurunca, which was taken by the 5th Army on 3 November 1943. At the front of the column is a Daimler Mk II armoured car, which had a main armament of a 2-pounder gun in the turret and a Besa 7.92 machine gun mounted coaxially. (*Author's Collection*)

Above: This 8th Army QF 3.7-inch Mk III anti-aircraft gun is being prepared to fire against German ground targets in November 1943. The ten-man crew of the British gun are folding out its legs while others look for the air burst shells used against ground forces. Although this standard medium anti-aircraft gun had been designed in the 1920s and early 1930s, it did not appear until 1936. *(Author's Collection)*

Right: Men of the Grave Registration Service take the body of a US soldier of the 30th Infantry Division to be buried as his comrades look on respectfully, on 2 November 1943. He has been killed in the advance on the town of Pietravairano and will now be interred beside other casualties of the battle. Even as the fighting continued, the GRS had to fulfil their task of burying the dead and marking the graves, which were to be dealt with after the war. *(Author's Collection)*

Right: Mules were not only used to bring supplies up to the front by the Allied armies, they were also utilised to bring wounded back to military hospitals. The men being taken back for treatment by an Indian soldier have been wounded during fighting along the Sangro River. Fighting along the river was an attempt by the 5th Army to penetrate the Bernhardt Line, which was an extension of the more substantial Gustav Line. Fighting along the Sangro lasted from 20 November to 4 December 1943, and ended with the successful Allied crossing of the river. (*Author's Collection*)

Below: General Sir Bernard Montgomery in the centre is photographed with Lieutenant General Sir Oliver Leese, CBE, DSO, who has just succeeded him as C-in-C of the 8th Army. On the left of Montgomery is Lieutenant General Herbert Lumsden, DSO, MC. General Montgomery left his command in Italy on 23 December 1943 and was then involved in preparations for Operation Overlord, the Allied invasion of Normandy, in June 1944. He was put in command of 21st Army Group, which made up the majority of the British contribution to Overlord. General Herbert Lumsden did not survive the war, being killed in the Pacific War during a Japanese kamikaze attack on the aircraft carrier USS *New Mexico*. His death, on 5 January 1945, gave him the dubious honour of being the highest-ranking British officer killed in action in the Second World War. (*Author's Collection*)

Two Italian soldiers of the Bersaglieri light infantry fighting for the Allied armies in late 1943 chat to US soldiers while one shows the damaged breech of his Carcano Model 38 carbine to them. In the early days of Italian co-operation with the US and British campaign, the pro-Allied troops wore their old uniforms. The other Italian, who seems rather disinterested by the exchange, is better armed with a Beretta 1938A sub-machine gun. (*US National Archives*)

In a tragic scene, Captain W.D. Giffen, a medical officer of the Hampshire Regiment, checks the bandages of Quartermaster Sergeant F. Clements in December 1943. The sergeant had sustained horrific burns to his head when the petrol lorry he was driving was hit by German shellfire. Although the troops who performed second-line roles were deemed to be safer than their frontline comrades, they still suffered heavy casualties during the campaign. (*Author's Collection*)

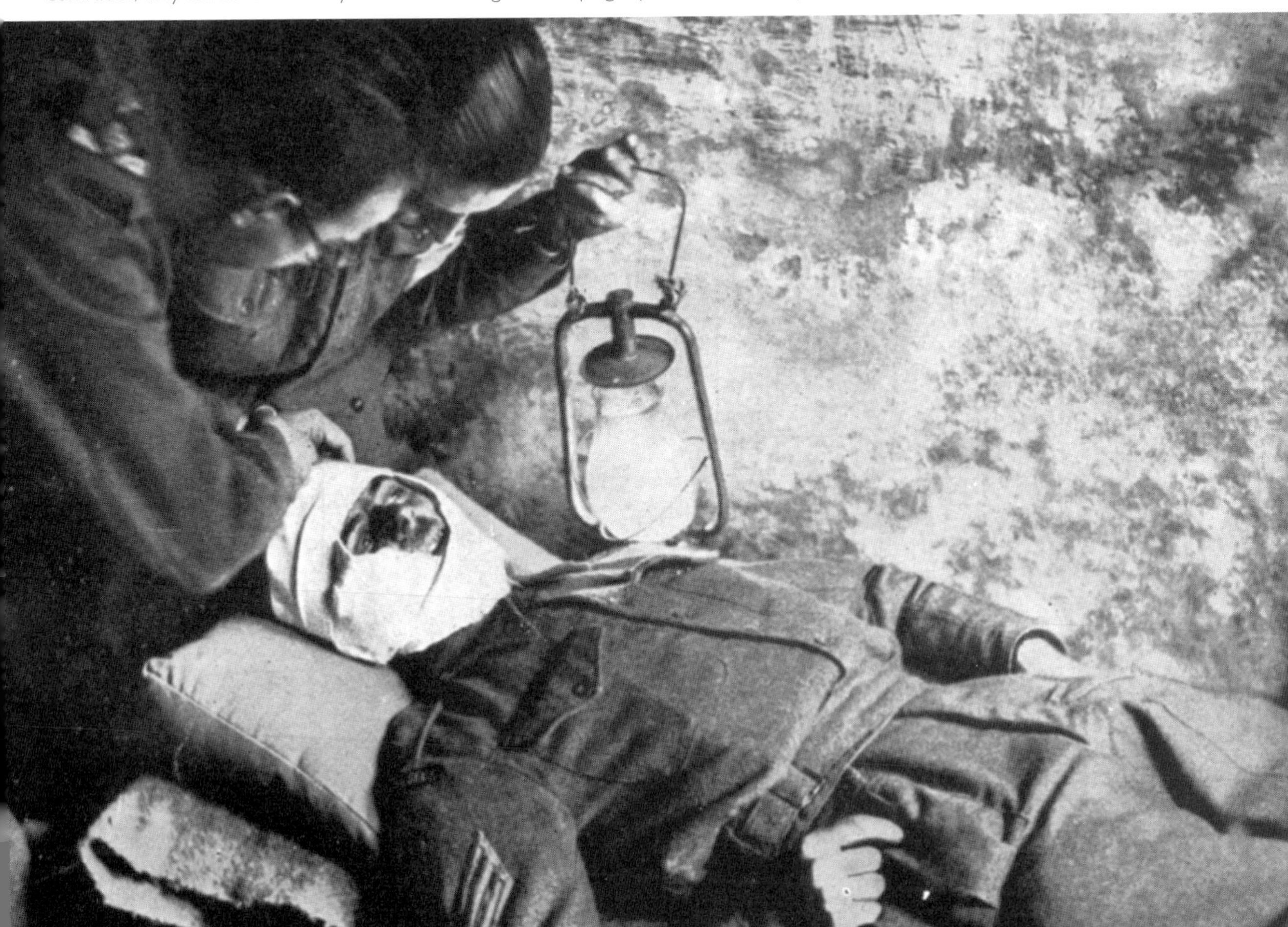

A dispatch rider of the 5th Army is totally bogged down by the mud following a long period of heavy rain. It was one of those annoying myths that circulate in wartime that the men of the 5th and 8th armies were busy 'sunbathing' in Italy. Jokes and taunts by the public and soldiers serving in northern France and other theatres from 1943 did not go down well with men serving on the Italian Front. Presumably, this comparison was made strongly by the German soldiers fighting on the Russian Front to their comrades in Italy. (*Author's Collection*)

A Canadian infantryman peers around a wall of an abandoned house on the road to the town of San Leonardo. He is on high alert as a counter-attack to retake the town has just begun by the Germans, who had been pushed out of San Leonardo. The so-called Moro River Campaign lasted from early December 1943 to 4 January 1944. It was fought between the German 76th Panzer Corps and four infantry divisions and two brigades of tanks. Allied casualties during the campaign were heavy, with troops from the Empire suffering greatly: 2,339 Canadians, 1,600 New Zealanders and 3,400 Indians died in the fighting. (*Author's Collection*)

Two British soldiers of the US 5th Army look towards Monte Camino in early December 1943, dressed for winter fighting. The strategic mountain had been fought over in early November, with fighting going on from the 5th to the 11th. Just less than a month later, the US 5th Army is about to launch a second attack, which would be fought from 2 to 5 December. The German positions were part of the Bernhardt Line, which formed the last line of defence before the greater defences of the Gustav Line. *(Author's Collection)*

A determined-looking Bren gunner of the 56th 'London' Infantry Division of the US 5th Army sits in his slit trench on the road to Monte Camino in early December 1943. The 56th did not fight in the Sicilian Campaign but landed at Salerno as part of the British X Corps. It took part in the fighting for Monte Cassino and along the Gustav Line, serving there during January and February 1944. After being withdrawn for rest and reorganisation to British bases in Egypt, the division arrived back in Italy in July 1944, fighting against the German Gothic Line. *(Author's Collection)*

Three soldiers of the US 3rd Infantry Division enjoy a Christmas dinner on 25 December 1943. During late 1943, it was noted that Allied morale was suffering from the harder-than-expected progress in Italy. In an attempt to raise the morale, special 'comfort boxes' were sent to every American soldier fighting in Italy. These soldiers are using the bonnet of their jeep, with the Allied white star decal, as a table to enjoy the chicken dinner they have been served. They also have a large pack of cigarettes to share when they go back into the front line later in the day. (*US Army Archives*)

This fine photograph shows a unit of Indian troops supported by a Universal Gun Carrier, which is armed not only with a Bren gun but also with a captured German MG42. The unit of the 6th Royal Frontier Force appears to have a mixture of Hindus and Sikhs as two of the soldiers are wearing turbans, as prescribed by their religion. In the foreground of the photograph is a 3-inch mortar getting ready to give covering fire for the gun carrier as it moves forward. They are fighting between Lanciano and Orsogna alongside New Zealand troops as they battle to take German positions along the Sango River in December 1943. (*Author's Collection*)

Sherman tanks move through the ruins of the town of Ortona, which finally fell to the Canadian troops on 28 December 1943. The German defenders of the town were made up mainly of the 1st Parachute Division under the command of Lieutenant General Richard Heinrich. Canadian troops of the 1st Infantry Division finally took the town after eight days of battle, losing 2,500 casualties during the fighting. Ortona was an insignificant port on the Adriatic coast and the troops who took it were untested, which no doubt added to their high casualty rate. *(Author's Collection)*

Two brothers, Private 1st Class Heinz and Private Frank Schorling from Jersey City, man a Browning M1917 heavy machine gun on New Year's Eve 1943. They are fighting in the Venafro area and their machine gun is a First World War era Browning M1917A1. Although outdated by the Second World War, the M1917 was reliable and remained in frontline service until 1945. *(US Army Archives)*

A small 100-strong unit of Belgian commandos, known as the 4th Troop of the 10th Inter-Allied Commando, were sent to Italy in November 1943. This unit was posted along a 3-mile stretch of the Sangro River and stayed there for several months before being transferred to occupied Yugoslavia. In Yugoslavia they co-operated with British-trained Yugoslavian commandos but political differences between the men and the Communist partisans led to its disbandment. (*Author's Collection*)

A group of German prisoners is brought into Allied lines by a mixture of British and Indian troops after the battle for Moro River. The fighting around the Moro lasted from 4 December 1943 to 4 January 1944. This month-long battle was fought between two infantry divisions and two armoured brigades of the 8th Army and a Panzer division, a Parachute division and two Panzergrenadier divisions of the German 76th Panzer Korps. (*Author's Collection*)

A platoon of the Canadian Seaforth Highlanders from the 1st Canadian Infantry Division prepare to move from the temporary cover of a ruined farmhouse. They are fighting at San Leonardo during the Moro River Campaign, which lasted from 4 December 1943 to 4 January 1944. Their officer looks towards German lines with his binoculars before sending his men forward. The Canadian Highlanders had fought in Sicily and crossed over to mainland Italy on 3 September and by 25 October, were fighting towards the Moro River. *(Author's Collection)*

Smiling Canadian Engineers walk towards the front line with several carrying mine detectors during the Moro River Campaign of December 1943 to January 1944. Their detectors are the standard No. 3, which was introduced to deal with the minefields laid by the Italians in 1940 in Libya. A newer type, the 4A, was in use with the British and Commonwealth service from 1942, just in time for the Battle of El Alamein. It was British Army Engineers who removed Axis mines to create a corridor for their troops to advance through. *(Author's Collection)*

This officer of the German paratroopers is brought into Allied lines along with a number of his comrades by a single Canadian soldier of the 8th Army. He has been captured during the fighting around Ortona on the Adriatic coast during the Moro River Campaign of December to January 43/44. German prisoners were often looked upon with curiosity or even in awe by their Allied captors. However, these Canadian soldiers look to be neither overawed nor intimidated by this prisoner, who has given up without a fight. (*Author's Collection*)

Chapter Five

January-May 1944
The Gustav Line

The German strategy for the defence of central and northern Italy relied heavily on a series of fortified defence lines that were being built or were planned to be built across the peninsula. It was decided to build three parallel lines slanting across the Italian peninsula, with each line being 7–11 miles apart. The Reinhardt Line, also known as the Winter Line, ran from the mouth of the Garigliano River in the west over the Abruzzi and along the Sangro River to the Adriatic coast. This first line was only a chain of light fieldworks that was the forward position of the German defence lines. It was occupied by German troops who had withdrawn from southern Italy and had been put into trenches to await the Allied attack. To the north of the Reinhardt Line was the more substantial Gustav Line, which was built across the Italian peninsula at its narrowest point. It followed the course of the Garigliano, the Rapido and the Gari rivers using these natural barriers to enhance the defences to full advantage. This second line of defence was built more substantially and included concrete pillboxes that were built in the river valley bottoms and along the ridges above them. The clever exploitation of the natural features and difficult terrain made the Gustav Line almost impenetrable. Hitler had put his faith in the Gustav Line and let it be known that it had to be held, saying: 'The Gustav Line must be held at all costs for the sake of the political consequences which would follow a completely successful defence. The Führer expects the bitterest struggle for every yard.' Near the western end of the Gustav Line lay the town and monastery of Cassino, which formed a strong bastion (*see* Chapter 6). To the south of the defence line ran the Rapido and Garigliano rivers, which gave the German defences an extra protection against an Allied advance from the south. As one commentator said describing the Gustav Line: 'The Garigliano and Rapido rivers formed the moat, the mountains the bastions, and Monte Cassino the guard tower of the gateway through which the road led to Rome.'

In late 1943 and early 1944, the Allied plan to move further northwards through Italy was constantly frustrated, largely by the difficult terrain of the country. The Germans could turn every hill and mountain into a fortress, and once each of these was taken, there was another hill and mountain beyond. The Germans proved to be masters of defence in Italy as well as in withdrawing from one defensive position to another in good order. In mid-January, the US 5th Army made its first attempt to cross the Rapido and Garigliano rivers forming the 'moat' of the Gustav Line. On 15 January, the US 2nd Corps launched an attack towards the Rapido River, taking Monte Trocchio, which was the last barrier before they reached it. On 20 January, the US 36th Division began an assault on the Garigliano River to the north of the Liri River. This was largely unsuccessful, with only the US 141st Infantry Regiment managing to cross the river. A few companies of the 143rd Regiment also managed to get across the river but these were wiped out by a German attack. The failure to establish a bridgehead on the north bank of the Garigliano led to a halt to the offensive on 22 January. On 17 January, the British X Corp's artillery had opened up a bombardment on the German positions on the north bank of the Garigliano River. Meanwhile on the right flank of the start line, the British 46th Division tried to gain control of the confluence of three rivers, the Liri, Rapido and Garigliano. The British 56th Division made an attack in the centre of the front while on the left, the British 5th Division also moved forward. At 9.00 am on the same day, Operation Panther was launched with full-scale assaults across the Garigliano River by the 5th, 46th and 56th divisions. Two divisions, the 5th and 56th, successfully crossed the river but the 46th failed to get its troops across. By the morning of the 18th, the 5th and 56th had established bridgeheads on the north bank of the Garigliano, pushing back the German 94th Division. German reinforcements were now rushed to stop the British advance, including the 90th Panzergrenadier Division and the 29th Armoured Division. Despite the arrival of German reinforcements, the 5th and 56th divisions widened their bridgeheads over the Garigliano and took the towns of Minturno and Castelforte. Their attempts to move further northwards were stopped by strong German resistance, but the various attacks by the 5th Army had had the desired effect. They took the German attention away from the site of the landings at Anzio, which began on 22 January. In total, the Germans moved three divisions from the coast to counter the US 5th Army's offensive. These first moves against the Gustav Line were the start of an almost four-month campaign that was to frustrate the Allied plans in Italy. After January, any attempts to put pressure on the Gustav Line usually resulted in little progress as the fighting around Cassino turned into a bloody stalemate. At no point during the four-month period of fighting was there any real chance of breaking the Gustav defences. The difficult terrain meant that Allied tanks could not be used in sufficient numbers to break the stalemate. All of the Allied effort was put into the fight for Cassino, and the German defenders along the Gustav Line were still holding firm.

However, by the spring of 1944, the decisive fighting for the Gustav Line was coming to an end and the first signs of weaknesses in the German resistance were showing. General Alexander now decided to finish the Germans off and moved all available 8th Army units closer to the front. During April and early May 1944, Alexander brought across most of the remainder of his 8th Army from their positions on the Adriatic coast. They were to be part of the full-scale offensive up the Liri Valley in the direction of the Italian capital. As the pressure built along the Gustav Line, any chance of breaking through its defences would entail bringing in a large number of fresh troops. The severe losses suffered by the Allied forces around Cassino meant that in May 1944, reinforcements were greatly needed. Four Free French divisions and three groups of irregular Moroccan Tabors were formed into the French Expeditionary Corps (FEF). Amongst other US and British units sent to the front were the Polish 2nd Corps, which had been formed in the Middle East in 1941. Before the launch of the final offensive against Cassino, these forces were reorganised, with the 2nd Polish being deployed to the north of the town. A combined force of the 13th British Division and the 2nd Canadian Corps was situated in the centre and the FEF was on the left flank. The US 2nd Corps was deployed on the Tyrrhenian coast while the 8th Army was spread out behind the Garigliano River. The 8th Army's 10th Corps was at the Garigliano and the 5th, made up of the 6th South African Armoured Division and the 21st Tank Brigade, was on the Adriatic coast to the east. Ready to support the move to the north were the US 5th Army's 6th Corps, which could break out of the Anzio bridgehead. In total, the Allies now had twenty-eight divisions, with the 5th Army having five, with four of these being Free French. The 8th Army had the equivalent of twelve divisions along the front with another six divisions still in the Anzio bridgehead. Another three divisions were in the Adriatic coastal region ready to move forward when the 8th Army began an offensive. Opposing the Allies were twenty-three German divisions, but these were widely dispersed by Kesselring, who did not know where the threat was coming from.

General Alexander expected that the Germans would hold on to the Gustav Line for as long as humanly possible. He knew, however, that other defence lines further north were being prepared for when the Gustav Line was broken. The plan to overcome the German defences was for the US VI Corps to break out from Anzio and join with the offensive planned by the 8th Army and US 5th Army. Both Allied armies would advance from their bridgehead along the Garigliano River front across the Rapido River and then up the Liri Valley towards Rome. Hopefully, the Allied troops would trap the German 76th and 14th Panzer Corps, who were earmarked to man the defence lines further north. To the north of the Gustav Line between Cassino and Rome was another defence line, the Hitler Line, which was later named the Senger Line. This defence line was to provide a fallback position for any troops that were pushed out of the Gustav Line during the campaign.

The plan for the Allied May Offensive was that the US 5th Army, positioned south of the Liri River, would launch three thrusts. On the right of the front was the French Expeditionary Corps with the 2nd and 4th Moroccan divisions and 3rd Algerian Division, and the 1st French Motorised Division. These French units were good mountain troops and would move across the mountains from their base on the Garigliano River. Having crossed the rugged mountains, the French would move up the Ausente Valley to the Liri River and to Pontecorvo. On the left of the French were the US II Corps with the 85th and 88th divisions who would advance westwards and then northwards along the coast to Gaeta. In support of these advances, the troops in the Anzio beachhead were to break out and join in with the US II Corps. Coming from Anzio were the US VI Corps with the 3rd, 34th and 45th US Infantry divisions and the 1st Armoured Division. Also part of the Anzio force were two British divisions attached to the VI Corps, the 1st and 5th Infantry. The breakout force was to head for the eastern Alban Hills to the south of Rome through the Liri Valley.

The 8th Army's Polish contingent – II Corps with the 3rd Carpathian and 5th Kresowa divisions – were to cut off any withdrawing Germans from the fighting for Cassino (*see* Chapter 6). They were to join up with the British XIII Corps, which would have advanced up the Liri Valley. II Polish Corps would then deal with the defenders of Cassino and Monastery Hill before heading towards the Hitler Line. XIII Corps with the British 4th and 78th Infantry divisions, 8th Indian Infantry Division and 6th Armoured Division were to cross the Rapido River just to the south of Cassino. Once across the river they would advance up the Liri Valley to facilitate the advance of the Canadian I Corps. They would allow the Canadians, with the 1st Canadian Infantry and 5th Canadian Armoured Division, to drive up the Liri Valley and break through the Hitler Line. The British X Corps, which only had a single division, the New Zealand, was to move through the mountains to the east of the Polish II Corps. This movement would not be made until the Poles had moved forward towards the Hitler Line. Other Allied formations were to act as reserves for the offensive, with the 6th South African Armoured Division in direct reserve. There was also another force on the Adriatic coast made up of the V Corps – 4th and 10th Indian Infantry divisions – and an Italian Co-Belligerent Motorised brigade.

By mid-May, it was becoming obvious that the German control of the Gustav Line had become untenable. Despite a delaying action on the Hitler Line, from 19 to 23 May, the Germans had little choice but to fall slowly back towards Rome. On 23 May, the Anzio beachhead forces entered the battle in earnest, beginning a major attack that aimed to cut across the 10th Army's line of retreat. On the 26th, however, General Clark switched his main axis of attack north-westwards, towards Rome, and abandoned any real effort to cut off the 10th Army. With the 8th Army becoming badly bogged down in traffic jams in the Liri Valley, and the more mobile French denied permission to cut in front of the 8th Army, the Germans were able to slowly pull back ahead of the Allied spearheads. Though Rome fell to the 5th Army on 4 June, very few German troops were intercepted.

The British XIII Corps with the 4th British and 8th Indian divisions leading managed to cross the Rapido River. Although they established bridgeheads on the opposite bank, they came under constant pressure by the Germans. At the same time, the 5th Army's 'French Expeditionary Corps' took Monte Majo and their 1st Motorised Division moved quickly up the west bank of the Garigliano River. They captured two towns, Sant'Ambrogio and Sant'Appollinare, which meant the west bank of the river was now clear of German troops. Along the Rapido, the British XIII Corps made progress against the German defences from 14 May, with support from the 78th Division. While the 13th was advancing, the rest of the 5th Army was advancing northwards and the French Goumier irregular troops were moving across the mountains to the west of the main front. In total, six Allied divisions were now involved in the offensive and were faced by two struggling German divisions. On 15 May, the XIII Corps reached the Cassino–Pignataro road and the Canadian Corps was brought up to the front to exploit Allied successes. By 18 May, Kesselring was desperately trying to plug the gaps being forced by the Allied troops. He sent reinforcements to the Gustav Line but they arrived piecemeal and were wasted in a series of desperate counter-attacks. Although the Hitler Line was still holding, the general situation along the Gustav Line was only going one way. The Gustav Line had finally crumbled, but not without a heavy cost to the Allied armies. During the offensive the Germans had had ten divisions destroyed and had effectively lost two armies.

Soldiers of the British X Corps are seen on the Garigliano Front in mid-January 1944 probing the defences of the Gustav Line. The first assaults on the German defences were a failure and it became apparent that it would take weeks or even months to break through them. This well-armed patrol unusually has two Thompson sub-machine guns, while their comrade prepares to throw a Mills grenade. (*NARA*)

The Royal Navy supported the Allied campaign with naval bombardments to relieve the pressure on ground forces. These RN ratings have been put ashore on the Garigliano Front in late January 1944 to receive information from reconnaissance planes to co-ordinate their ship's fire. Co-operation between the 8th and 5th armies and the Allied air forces and Royal Navy often proved decisive during the Italian Campaign. *(Author's Collection)*

During a series of attempts to cross the Rapido River to the south of Cassino, two US soldiers set up smoke pots to screen their comrades from German fire. The first attempt was made on 20 January, which failed, and was followed over the next few days by further costly failures. By the 22nd, all assault boats had been destroyed, and a day later, the attacks in that sector were halted. Casualties during a few days of fighting were heavy, with 143 killed, 663 wounded and 875 reported missing. *(US Army Archives)*

US troops fire their 81mm mortar towards German positions along the Rapido River to the south of the Gustav Line. The photograph was taken on 24 January, when the US 5th Army finally made a successful crossing of the river. After three days of costly failures, the Americans had switched their attacks to another sector and were successful. On the 27th, the Americans got a few tanks across the river to support an advance to the north of Monte Cassino. (*US Army Archives*)

A German Mörser 18 21cm heavy howitzer is seen dug in along the Gustav Line in early 1944 as the front stabilised. The Mörser 18 was a large gun to transport, especially in the difficult terrain of the Italian peninsula. German production had been switched to the lighter 17cm from 1942, although this gun remained in Wehrmacht service until the end of the war. (*Author's Collection*)

This German machine-gun crew have set up their position in the flooded territory on the edge of the Pontine Marshes in early 1944. During the fighting along the German defence line from January to May, most of the battles were fought around Cassino. However, the Germans had to be prepared to try to counter any assaults by the US 5th and 8th armies along the whole front. *(Author's Collection)*

British soldiers rest after a patrol in an ancient Roman amphitheater, which is being used as a bivouac to provide some shelter for them. The soldier sleeping on a bench is resting his head against the plinth of a Roman statue, with his boots ready if he needs to put them on in a hurry. This unit is fighting on the Garigliano Front in February 1944, which was part of the early Allied attempts to penetrate the German-held Gustav Line. *(Author's Collection)*

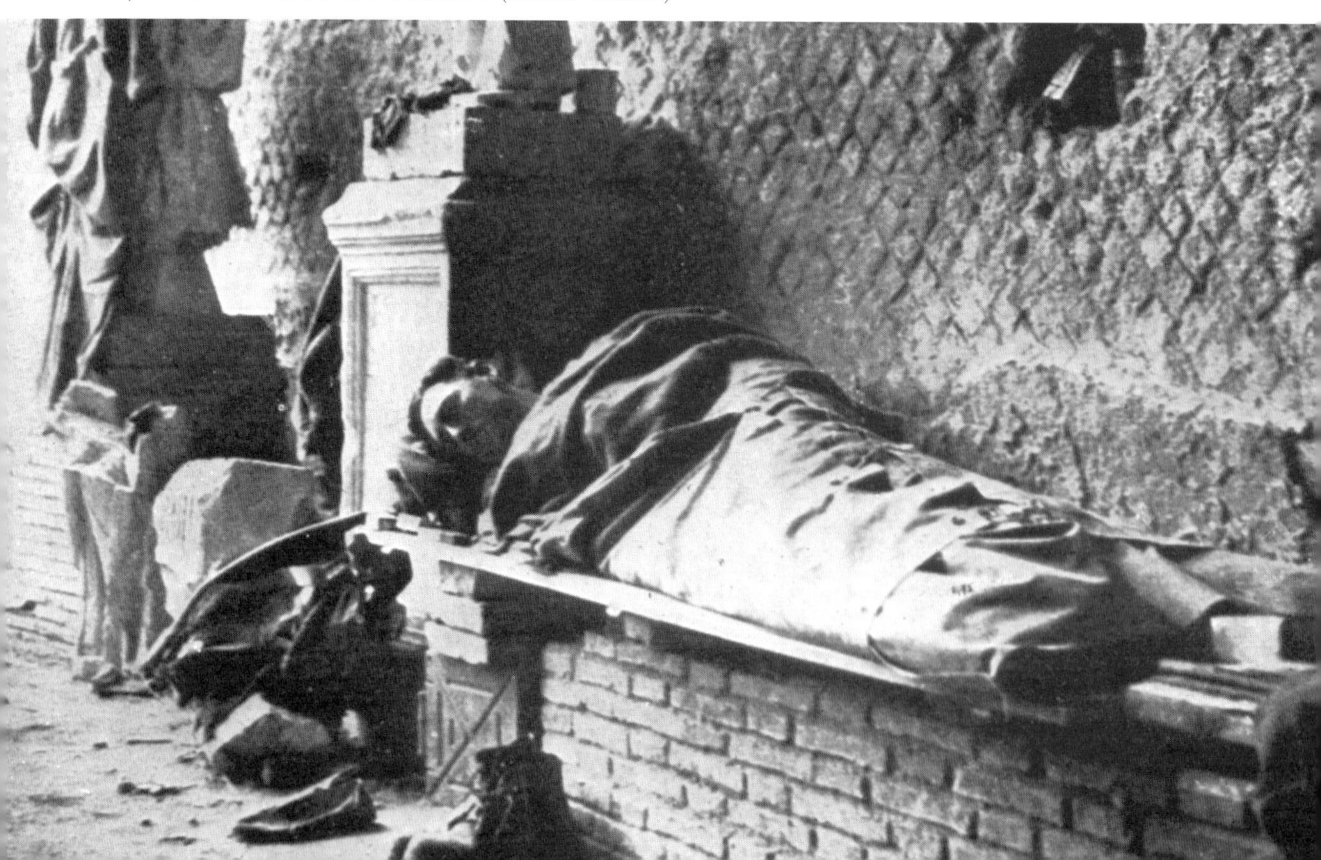

Three Nepalese Gurkhas of the Indian Army chat about a recent encounter with the enemy. On the left of the group is Lance Naik, Okel Gurung, who a few days before this photograph was taken had captured a German machine-gun nest single-handedly. Gurkhas were fine soldiers who were renowned for their valour, but they were not supermen and at times suffered heavy casualties due to their military naivety. (*Author's Collection*)

Heavy military traffic on the muddy roads of central Italy in February 1944 turned most already poor roads into quagmires. A Canadian Sherman M4 tank had moved to the side of the road to let other traffic pass but it skidded and slipped into a ditch. Its crew will attempt to pull their tank out with the help of another M4 using steel cables, while on the other side of the road a Bren Gun Carrier struggles through the mud. *(Author's Collection)*

This 5th Army Priest M7 self-propelled 105mm howitzer has been moved up to Monte Marrone to support an attack on the German-held position in late March 1944. The defensive positions held by the Germans controlled the road from the towns of Colti and Arina. Its crew look relaxed under the cover of a camouflage net and have thirteen shells ready for when ordered to open fire. *(Author's Collection)*

Left: This photograph of a German 100mm Kanone K18 firing in defence of the Gustav Line was taken on 12 March 1944. The blowback from the breech and the smoke coming from the barrel shows the gun at the moment of firing. The K18 was described as being too heavy to move with horses and too light for its modest shell weight. (*Author's Collection*)

Below: French soldiers of the US 5th Army take a ride on one of their M10 tank destroyers as they move northwards in early May 1944. These US-made armoured vehicles had been supplied to the 'French Expeditionary Corps' along with M8 tank destroyers. They have halted at the side of a road to allow a local Italian farmer to pass with his oxcart full of hay. (*Author's Collection*)

A heavy artillery unit of a French Colonial division fires its US-supplied heavy howitzer against German positions in early May 1944. Their gun is a French-designed M1918 155mm, which was supplied to the US Army during the First World War. Some of these guns were still in service with the USA in the Second World War and were issued to the French in Italy. (*Author's Collection*)

French troops move up a road past a destroyed German StuG III tank destroyer towards the Gustav Line. It was the French Expeditionary Corps that finally broke through the German defences on 11 May 1944. Two of the soldiers carry large shovels, which will be used to make repairs to the road as they move up into the hills and then to dig trenches and other dugouts when they reach the front line. *(Author's Collection)*

A truck of the French Expeditionary Corps under the command of General Alphonse Juin moves up the road towards the Gustav Line. It pulls a French M1897 field gun, which has a camouflage netting hanging over it, along with branches to be used in constructing a shelter. To the right of the truck, the infantry column includes a soldier who has commandeered a horse to carry him. Although the advance of the French troops looks a little disorganised, when these soldiers got into the front line they proved to be formidable fighters. *(Author's Collection)*

Right: Algerian Goumiers – muleteers of the French Expeditionary Corps – move steadily up a mountain path to cross the Aurunci Mountains in early May. The mule train passes an M8 howitzer motor carriage with a 75mm gun, which was mounted on the chassis of an M5 Stuart light tank. As this vehicle was being replaced in US service, some M8s were handed over to the French Expeditionary Corps in Italy. (*US Army Archives*)

Below: Dead German paratroopers of the Hermann Göring Division lie in a flooded gully during fighting in the vicinity of the Gustav Line. They have been trying to use the gully as cover for their attack on the Allies' positions in the Pontine Marshes. The marshes had been drained by Mussolini's Fascist regime, which greatly reduced the occurrence of malaria in central Italy. In 1943, the Germans decided to flood the Pontine Marshes to delay Allied advances. Due to the resulting rise in the deadly disease, this has been described as an act of biological warfare. (*Author's Collection*)

A British Army patrol rests at the side of a railway track during the early days of the May Offensive. They are waiting for the order to move up to the front as their engineers are preparing a bridge across the Liri River. General Alexander had issued a communiqué to his troops in English, Polish, French and Italian, which said: 'Today the bad days are behind us and tomorrow we can see the victory ahead.' (*Author's Collection*)

In the first hours of the May Offensive, Signallers of the Royal Artillery watch their comrades cross the Garigliano River. After the failure of attempts to cross the river in January 1944, the 8th and US 5th Army were much better prepared to succeed this time. Some of the 8th Army's personnel had served in the North African desert since 1940 and then fought in Sicily before landing in southern Italy. (*Author's Collection*)

A 25-pounder field gun of the Polish II Corps is dug in on the approaches to the town of Piedimonte in late May 1944. The Polish had breached the Hitler Line on 24 May alongside the 1st Canadian and 5th Canadian Armoured divisions. Hitler Line joined the Gustav Line after running from Terracina through the Aurunci Mountains and the two defence lines met at Monte Cairo. (*NAC*)

Soldiers of the Polish II Corps drag a German officer out of a trench on the outskirts of Piedimonte on 26 May. The town, which is to the north-west of Cassino, saw several days of heavy fighting that an eyewitness described as 'bitter'. Most Polish soldiers had been released from Soviet captivity in Siberia after 1941. They had been held there since the Soviet invasion of Poland in September 1939. (*Author's Collection*)

In fighting for Monte Majo and the town of Castelforte, these German soldiers were taken prisoner by Free French troops. Two hundred Germans were captured during the fighting and have been put into a barbed wire enclosure while they are questioned by Allied officers. During the Italian Campaign, the Germans fought well and only surrendered when there was no alternative. *(Author's Collection)*

M4 Sherman tanks undergo some trials before going back to the front line on 25 May 1944. They have been repaired and handed over to a replacement crew, who are putting their tanks through their paces. Tanks were expensive to build and every effort was made by US recovery crews to put them back into action. (*US Army Archives*)

Chapter Six

January-May 1944
The Battles for Cassino

In January 1944, the first major Axis defensive line running across Italy, the Gustav Line, was being threatened by gathering Allied forces of the 8th and 5th armies. The Gustav Line, also known as the Winter Line, was dominated by the town of Cassino, which was situated at the junction of the Liri and Rapido rivers. Above the town was the hilltop Benedictine monastery Monte Cassino, which dated back to AD 529. Although the Germans were camped around the monastery, they had not occupied the building but were dug in on the slopes surrounding it. Monte Cassino's strategic position meant that it and the town below had to be taken to allow the Allied northwards advance to continue. It was being used as an artillery spotting position as the Allied troops approached it, making the German artillery fire extremely accurate. So important was Monte Cassino to the fall of the Gustav Line that the battle to take it is often referred to as the 'Battle for Rome'. In order to conquer the Gustav Line it was essential that Cassino should be taken whatever the cost. From 17 January to 18 May 1944, a series of four major Allied assaults took place involving a multi-national Allied force. This force involved British, Americans, Polish, Free French, Canadians, New Zealanders, South Africans and pro-Allied Italians. In total, 240,000 Allied troops and nearly 1,900 tanks and 4,000 aircraft took part in the five-month campaign. Facing them were 140,000 German troops in what became a mammoth struggle for a small town and ruined monastery.

By 7 January, German units had established defensive positions at the far end of the Liri Valley in the mountains overlooking the town of Cassino. At the start of the fighting for Cassino, the garrison comprised the 44th Infantry Division, reinforced by part of the 71st Infantry Division. In addition, General von Senger und Etterlin, the new commander of the 14th Panzer Corps, had sent a battlegroup from 90th Panzergrenadier Division based on the Garigliano River front to reinforce Cassino. Attacking Cassino were the US 5th Army, made up of the US 2nd and the British 10th Corps and the French Expeditionary Corps – 2nd Moroccan, 3rd Algerian, 3rd and 4th Groups of Tabors and the 2nd Armoured Group, and a reserve that included the Italian Co-Belligerent 1st Motorised Corps.

The first Allied movements against Cassino began on 4–5 January 1944 with the intention of diverting German forces from threatening the Allied landings at Anzio (*see* Chapter 7). French troops outflanked Cassino and took up positions only 4 miles from the German defensive positions to the north of the town. They were joined by the US 6th Armoured Regiment, which took Monte Porchia above the town. By 23 January, the Allied armies were gathering around Cassino, with the French Expeditionary Corps and the US 34th Division moving north of the town. On 24 January, an attack against Monte Cassino began from the north-east led by the US 34th and 36th divisions. The Americans got to within a few hundred yards of the monastery but they suffered horrendous casualties. Bad weather then closed in and the attack petered out, and the surviving US troops returned to their start positions.

In early February, the 135th Regiment of the US 34th Division got to within 1,000 yards of Monte Cassino, taking some heights above the monastery. New attacks by the 135th and counter-attacks by the Cassino defenders ended on 6 February in total failure for the Americans. On the 11th, the 168th Regiment of the 34th tried to seize the monastery but were thrown back by the defenders. In mid-February, the forces around Cassino were heavily reinforced by three Allied divisions from the Adriatic Sector. These were the 2nd New Zealand, the 4th Indian Division and the 78th Infantry Division, forming the New Zealand Corps. With these fresh troops replacing the 168th, a second major attack on Cassino began on 15 February after a heavy bombing campaign when 1,400 bombs weighing 405 tons were dropped by the Allied air forces. In the aftermath of these attacks, General Alexander is quoted as having said: 'It seemed to me inconceivable that any troops should be left alive after eight hours of such terrific hammering.' A major attack was now launched by the 4th Indian Division, which was aimed at a small knoll – Hill 593, which was between their start positions and Cassino. On two successive nights, the Indians made attacks on the knoll, with the assaulting force losing heavy casualties. On the 18th, there were three attempts to take the knoll but any troops that managed to reach the top were killed by heavy German fire. One Indian brigade bypassed the knoll and ended up in a valley that the German defenders had sown with mines. They had also sited their machine guns to create a killing zone, which forced the surviving Indians back to their starting positions. Meanwhile, New Zealand troops heading for Cassino crossed the Rapido River to the south of the town. German tanks attacked the New Zealand bridgehead and forced them back across the river. The tough German troops defending Cassino continued to resist the sporadic Allied assaults. The Germans turned the rubble from the now flattened town and monastery into improvised fortresses. In late February, General von Senger und Etterlin took advantage of a lull in the fighting to replace the exhausted battlegroup from the 90th Panzergrenadier Division with the fresh 1st Parachute Division. For the remainder of the fight for Cassino, the German paratroopers were the main defence force. The division's Machine Gun Regiment defended Cassino railway station while the 3rd Regiment held Cassino town and Monastery Hill, and the 4th Regiment defended the sector to the west and north of Cassino.

A third Allied attack against Cassino began on 15 March, with the 4th Indian Division moving down from its positions to the north of Cassino. They made steady progress and by the next day, they were two thirds of the way up the slope around Monte Cassino. For the first time, tanks were to be used in large numbers by the New Zealand Corps armoured force. M3 light tanks and M4 medium tanks of the 2nd New Zealand Division advanced up the slope to the summit of Monte Cassino. It had taken two days to get the tanks into position due to the cratered terrain they were trying to traverse. In addition, the New Zealand Infantry did not provide infantry support and the attack faltered. However, the assault did achieve some success, with new positions established around Monte Cassino. Further success was evident in Cassino town, with the New Zealanders gaining control of most of its ruins. While the week-long direct attack by the 2nd Division was underway, the 'French Expeditionary Corps' North African troops were skilfully moving across the mountains to envelop the German defences. After a week of fighting, the attack ended and the French and New Zealanders concentrated on bolstering the positions they had taken. Throughout the rest of March, the poor weather heavily affected the fighting, but the Allies kept up the pressure, with 1,200 tons of shells fired at Cassino as well as 1,000 tons of bombs from the air. A desperate stalemate now existed all along the Gustav Line, especially at Cassino and around the Anzio beachhead. The Allies were unable to overcome the German defence line and take Cassino while the Germans were equally unable to throw the forces in the Anzio beachhead 'back into the sea'. The losses during the March fighting were heavy, with the Allies suffering 2,400 casualties. The Indian Division suffered more than 1,100 losses, while the New Zealanders lost 1,160 men. Winston Churchill was frustrated at the lack of progress on the Gustav Line, particularly around Cassino. He asked Alexander why so many resources had been expended on a 2–3 mile front, with the equivalent of 5–6 divisions worn out in the fighting.

During April and May 1944, Alexander brought most of the remainder of the 8th Army across from the Adriatic coast. He was building up his forces for a final full-scale offensive against the Gustav Line up the Liri Valley and along the Garigliano River front. The offensive began on 11 May and included new assaults by the Polish II Corps against Cassino. Their attack began at 11.00 pm, when 2,000 guns of the 5th and 8th armies bombarded the German defences. At dawn the next day, large numbers of medium bombers of the Allied Tactical Air Force began bombarding the German positions. These bombardments were followed by a Polish and British attack to the north of Cassino, which was initially thrown back. During fighting on the 12th, the Polish attackers suffered 20 per cent losses in the first ninety minutes of the assault. On the 18th, the Poles, under the command of General Anders, launched the final, and eventually successful, attack against Monte Cassino. German soldiers of the 71st Infantry Division had been forced back and had scattered during the battle, and 2,000 were taken prisoner. Paratroopers continued to hold on but during the night, they received instructions to withdraw from Monte Cassino. Both sides were now totally exhausted and most of the Germans were able to get away from the battlefield and withdraw to the north.

Troops of the French Expeditionary Corps on the approaches to the battlefield of Monte Cassino fire their light anti-aircraft gun at German planes. The gun is a water-cooled version of the Browning M2 .50 heavy machine gun, which was usually used in an anti-aircraft role. Some of these guns were fitted with anti-aircraft sights but this one still lacks these and is being fired using the standard sights. *(Author's Collection)*

Men of the US Army's 100th Battalion raised from the Japanese population of Hawaii move towards the battle for Cassino in January 1944. The suspicions against the Japanese immigrant population of the USA had led to their mass internment in camps. Any men wanting to join the US Armed Forces initially had their papers stamped IV-C – 'Unacceptable for service due to ancestry'. Despite their treatment, there were many so-called Nisei willing to fight for their adoptive country. In January 1943, 10,000 volunteers came forward; training began in April but was delayed due to the continuing doubt about their loyalty. The 10th Battalion finally landed in Salerno, Italy, in September 1943 and fought its first battle fighting along the Volturno River in November. They then fought bravely at Monte Cassino, gaining the honourable nickname 'The Purple Heart Battalion'. Out of the 1,300 Nisei that landed in Italy, only 521 were left to fight in the aftermath of the Cassino Campaign. (*Author's Collection*)

Left: Using a bush for cover, a German artillery spotter looks for suitable targets for his battery in the battle for Cassino in March 1944. The accurate artillery fire from the German guns around the Cassino battleground caused heavy casualties amongst Allied troops. German gun crews were able to conceal their artillery in the ruins of Cassino and Monte Cassino after the heavy Allied air forces bombing of March. (*NAC*)

Below: Two German soldiers have established a shelter in the ruins of the heights of Monte Cassino during the siege by Allied forces in early February 1944. They have built a shelter of sorts using the camouflaged tarpaulin sections, which under better circumstances were designed to make a conventional tent. During shelling, this kind of shelter could become a death trap, with falling masonry killing many troops on both sides. In one such incident, a number of British soldiers were buried alive under the rubble and their comrades rushed to rescue them. A de facto truce was immediately called and Germans emerged from their foxholes to help their enemy dig them out in a rare example of humanity in war. (*NAC*)

The 83-year-old Abbot of Cassino monastery, Dom Gregorio Diamare, is escorted from his residence by German General von Senger und Etterlin on 16 February. This action was taken after the first Allied bombing of Cassino, with some bombs hitting Monte Cassino. German troops had moved the treasures of the monastery to safety and then onward to the Vatican in Rome. They wanted any bombing of the holy site to be seen as a war crime by the Allied air forces, giving the Germans a propaganda victory. (*Author's Collection*)

The crew of a MG42 machine gun fire across the rubble-strewn ruins of Cassino, which formed the battlefield for most of the five months of fighting. In February, the German 3rd Battalion of the 2nd Parachute Regiment of the 1st Parachute Division held a vital position known as 'Calvary Mount' against a strong US force from the 34th Division. (*Author's Collection*)

A German soldier rushes to help his comrades re-attach the shed track of a Panzer IV H tank that has been damaged in fighting around Cassino. Armoured vehicles did not play a major role during the battles for Cassino due largely to the difficult terrain. The Allies did use a number of Sherman M4 tanks, while the German assault guns were from the Panzergrenadier regiments involved in the fourth battle for the town. (*NAC*)

A platoon of Fallschirmjägers are ready to go on patrol after arriving at Cassino in mid-February 1944. They are shoving spare stick grenades into the leather belts of their splinter camouflage smocks. Mutual respect between the combatants developed during the fighting for Cassino and Monte Cassino. During one short truce, the Allied troops loaned the Germans stretchers to move their wounded from the battlefield. They also gave some of their spare chocolate rations to the German wounded and the stretcher-bearers. (*Author's Collection*)

The so-called 'Green Devils', an elite unit of the German 1st Parachute Division, move through the partly ruined town of Cassino in late February 1944. Units of the US 34th Division advanced towards the Rapido River on 23 January in an effort to surround the German garrison holding Cassino and the strategic heights of Monte Cassino. Cassino town and the monastery on top of Monte Cassino were to become the focus for Allied and German efforts over the next few months. (*Author's Collection*)

This German paratrooper fires from an abandoned building towards Allied positions at Cassino armed with a Fallschirmjägergewehr 42 assault rifle with a box of stick grenades at hand. The FG 42, as it was known, was one of the first efforts by the Germans to produce an automatic rifle. It had been produced with the support of Hermann Göring, the head of the Luftwaffe, and was only to be issued to the Fallschirmjägers. It was not a great success, was expensive to manufacture, and was discovered to be too flimsy to fire the Mauser round it used. (*Author's Collection*)

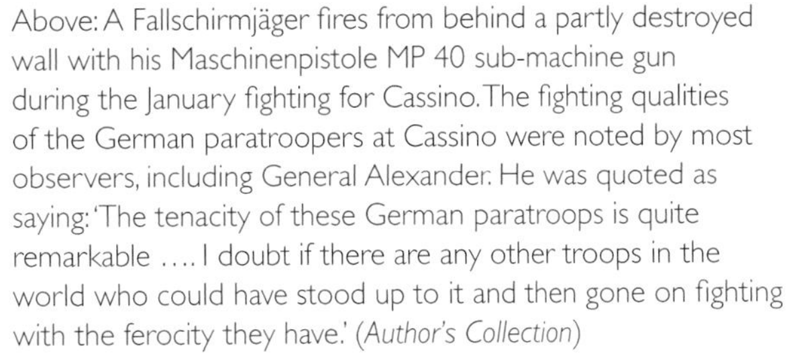

Above: A Fallschirmjäger fires from behind a partly destroyed wall with his Maschinenpistole MP 40 sub-machine gun during the January fighting for Cassino. The fighting qualities of the German paratroopers at Cassino were noted by most observers, including General Alexander. He was quoted as saying: 'The tenacity of these German paratroops is quite remarkable …. I doubt if there are any other troops in the world who could have stood up to it and then gone on fighting with the ferocity they have.' (*Author's Collection*)

Left: A single German paratrooper brings in captured US soldiers during the fighting around Cassino. They probably belong to the US 34th Division, which took part in the assault on the monastery on Monte Cassino in early February. When the Americans attacked the German positions, they were faced by hardened troops who had sown mines and booby traps and hidden barbed wire. The US troops overcame some of these obstacles but were eventually withdrawn from the attacks on Monte Cassino on 11 February. (*Author's Collection*)

The medieval monastery of Monte Cassino pictured in March 1944 after several months of fighting and artillery and air bombardments. Its ruins became a battleground as the German defenders dug in and dealt a heavy toll on the attacking Allied troops. Despite international appeals not to shell the monastery, the decision was made not to protect the historical site. Allied commanders sought the permission of Pope Pius XII to allow them to shell the monastery, which had a great religious significance to Catholics. (*Author's Collection*)

The devastated town of Cassino had been bombed on 15 March by a 500-strong Allied bomber force. The raid lasted three and a half hours, during which over 992 tons of bombs were dropped. A raid on 15 February that concentrated on Monte Cassino had seen 442 tons dropped. German casualties during the bombing raids were not as heavy as expected and when the ground war resumed, Allied attacks were met with stiff resistance. During the January to May 1944 campaign, 2,000 civilians were also killed in Cassino town and surrounding villages. (*Author's Collection*)

A paratrooper officer briefs his men of the 3rd Parachute Regiment before they go into action during the bitter fighting for Monte Cassino in March 1944. In most cases, the German officer led from the front and had the respect of the other ranks. The near disaster at Crete in which the Fallschirmjägers succeeded in their mission but suffered heavy casualties led to Hitler ordering no further launches of large-scale airborne operations. There were limited parachute operations in the Balkans but by mid-1944, only 30,000 of the 150,000 paratroopers in service were jump-qualified. (*NAC*)

Polish soldiers of the British 8th Army are seen in the rear area of the Italian Campaign showing their skills to their new commander, General Leese, in April 1944. He had taken over command of the 8th Army from General Montgomery in December 1943 and took charge of his men during the final attacks on Cassino in May 1944. Leese was a good leader but had issues with his US counterpart, General Clark, whom he was said to have disliked working with. The soldiers are showing the gathered audience how to pack and unpack a transport mule efficiently. (*Author's Collection*)

Italian Co-Belligerent troops fighting alongside the Allied armies fire their 75mm field gun towards German positions. In April 1944, the Italians fighting against the Germans were known as the 'Italian Liberation Corps'; 5,000 of these troops armed still with ex-Italian Army weapons and uniforms fought in battles around Monte Cassino. They fought well, suffering heavy casualties, and exposed the myth of Italian cowardice in battle. (*Author's Collection*)

In a break in fighting on the Cassino front in April 1944, an American artilleryman gives his British colleagues instruction in loading a US 155mm howitzer. It will take the strength of all four crewmen to lift the shell on its loading tray to push it into the breech of the gun. During the Italian Campaign, the US and Commonwealth troops of the 5th and 8th armies respectively fought a parallel offensive up the western and eastern coasts of Italy. (*Author's Collection*)

In late April, a Sturmgeschütz III Ausf. G assault gun of the '242 StuG Abt' moves across a stone bridge on the way to the battle for Cassino. The crew of the tank destroyer look up towards the distant heights of Monte Cassino in spring 1944. When they arrived in Cassino, the Sturmgeschütze appear to have been used defensively and were hidden in buildings and camouflaged. (*Cody Images*)

This British Army sniper from the Grenadier Guards aims at a German position in Cassino town. His sandbagged position provides him with some protection against the German snipers who are also operating in the ruins of the town. He is armed with a Lee Enfield .303 No. 4 (T) rifle, with the T signifying that it is fitted with a No. 32 telescopic sight. (*Author's Collection*)

Heavy machine-gunners of the 5th Army fire their Vickers .303 Mk I towards the German lines during the final weeks of the battle for Cassino in May 1944. This gun has a canvas cover over its water jacket to protect its crew from burning themselves when handling it. Although in service with the British Army since 1912, the Vickers remained in use until the 1960s due to its reliability. *(Author's Collection)*

New Zealand troops have captured a German PAK 40 anti-tank gun and have turned it against its former owners. In mid-March, the 24th, 25th and 26th battalions of the 6th Brigade went into action around Cassino. In this picture, they are attempting to fire at a German position on the high ground above them and will have to learn how to raise the gun's elevation. (*Author's Collection*)

A Thompson sub-machine-gunner of the 2nd New Zealand Division fires from behind the dubious cover of a pile of rubble to the south of Cassino. He is armed with the 1928 A1 model of the Thompson, which was the same type used by the gangsters of 1920s America. The New Zealand 2nd Division was under the command of the veteran of the Battle for Crete in 1941, Lieutenant General Freyberg. As part of the 5th Army it took part in two of the major assaults on Monte Cassino and then moved up to attack the Gustav Line. (*Author's Collection*)

New Zealand infantrymen stand guard over a group of German paratroopers whom they have captured during the battle for Cassino town. Although German Fallschirmjägers were known as tough fighters, the fighting for Cassino was to test all involved. The Sherman M4 tank provides cover for the captives and captors as the battle for Monte Cassino continues. (*Author's Collection*)

Left: This British Army ML 3-inch mortar, seen here with its Canadian crew in the hills around Cassino, has had its tube extended in an experiment by the Canadians to try to increase its range. Its crewmen and other soldiers protect their ears from the blast of the mortar while sitting amongst cases carrying 10lb bombs. Mortars were well suited to the kind of fighting going on around the town and the ruined monastery above it. (*Author's Collection*)

Below: This Italian paratrooper of the 'Nembo' Parachute Division of the Co-Belligerent forces holds a mountaintop position during fighting in May 1944. His unit belongs to the 22,000-strong Corpo Italiano di Liberazione, which was formed from a hardcore of former personnel of the pre-1943 'Nembo' Division. Although fighting alongside the Allied armies, these men had to make do with out-of-date Italian armaments. The paratrooper is armed with a 6.5mm Breda Model 30 light machine gun, which would soon be cast aside when better Allied arms were issued. (*Author's Collection*)

Moroccan Goumiers man a M1919A4 medium machine gun from the ruins of a wrecked house in the Cassino sector. They belong to the 2e Division d'Infanterie Marocaine, which was formed on 1 May 1943. The division arrived in Italy at the end of November the same year and fought in the push to advance to the German Gustav Line. Their machine gun was supplied to the Free French by the USA, who were initially reluctant to arm them. These mountain troops, however, proved themselves in North Africa in 1942 and the Sicilian Campaign, and 6,000 fought alongside partisans in Corsica from September 1943. (*Author's Collection*)

This 81mm mortar crew is manned by Moroccan Goumiers, who wear US M1917 helmets along with their native *djellaba* overcoat with a hood. The large hood was often used to carry rations, especially where other bags and haversacks were not issued. These men proved to be formidable mountain combatants and were happy to fight at close quarters with daggers and knuckle-dusters. (*Author's Collection*)

Right: General Alphonse Juin (1888–1967) had graduated from the École Spéciale Militaire in 1912. He served with Moroccan troops in 1914–18 and was badly wounded during the fighting, losing the use of one arm. After being captured in 1940, he was released from POW camp at the suggestion of the collaborationist Vichy Government and given command of their forces in North Africa. After the Allied invasion of North Africa in 1942, Juin joined the Free French and took command of the French Expeditionary Corps in Italy. His expertise in mountain warfare was a great advantage when his troops came to attack the Gustav Line. French troops were the first to penetrate the German defences using skills learnt during fighting in North Africa. (*Author's Collection*)

Below: Soldiers of the 5th Kresowa Infantry Division of the Polish II Corps are seen in action throwing their Mills grenades into German positions above Cassino in May 1944. They are under the command of General Wladyslaw Anders, who in March 1942 was put in charge of ex-POWs taken by the Russians in 1939. The Polish troops had been transported to Iran from the Soviet Union in 1942 and then reorganised to fight in Italy. Twenty-two thousand of their former officers had been secretly executed by the USSR at Katyn in April and May 1940, resulting in a shortage of men to command the Polish forces. (*Author's Collection*)

At the end of the battles for Cassino and Monte Cassino in May, a Polish-manned machine-gun position looks down on the battlefield. The four Allied assaults on the town and the monastery at Cassino from mid-January to mid-May 1944 involved up to 380,000 troops. While the Poles lost 1,000 men, the total casualties on the Allied side were 55,000 and the Germans lost at least 20,000. (*Author's Collection*)

In the aftermath of the German withdrawal from Cassino, the crypt of the convent chapel of Monte Cassino monastery is used as a shelter for Allied soldiers. During the height of the battle for Monte Cassino, the crypt took at least 100 direct hits, but it somehow withstood all of them. As the Germans retired to new defensive lines further north, the Allied troops were allowed time to recover from the battle. (*Author's Collection*)

Chapter Seven

January-May 1944
Anzio

As the winter set in early in 1943, the mountains that ran down the spine of Italy were soon covered in snow. The Allied advance from Salerno was soon bogged down, only 70 miles north of the port and well short of the German Gustav Line. Dominating the Gustav Line was Monte Cassino and the monastery that sat on top of the mountain. Rome was the objective of the Allied armies in southern and central Italy and the best route to the capital was up Route 6 along the Liri Valley. Several fast-flowing rivers also formed major barriers to the Allied advance and it looked like the campaign would soon turn into a costly stalemate. Having made several amphibious landings in southern Italy a few months before, the solution for the Allies appeared to be to bypass German defence lines by landing troops further north. The major problem for the Allies was the lack of suitable shipping as many of the ships used at Salerno and Taranto were now back in Britain waiting for the invasion of Normandy. Plans were now put in place to land substantial forces at the port of Anzio, 60 miles behind the Gustav Line. On 22 January 1944, Allied landings began at Anzio by the US VI Corps, with the 3rd US Division landing south of the town and the 1st British Division to the north. There was little German opposition to the landing and by midnight on the first day, 36,000 men and 5,000 Allied vehicles were ashore. By the next day, the number of troops landed had reached 50,000 and could now have pushed out of the bridgehead. For five vital days, the Allies made little attempt to break out from the bridgehead they had established at Anzio and the nearby town of Nettuno. The commander of the British 1st Division, General Penney, wanted to advance but was held back by his superior American officer, General Lucas. During this lull, large numbers of German troops were being moved by road towards the bridgehead to stop any breakout. Divisions from all four corners of Italy and beyond were already streaming towards Anzio. These included the 71st Division, which was just settling in on the Cassino front, and majority of the 3rd Panzergrenadier Division, field artillery battalions, heavy artillery, a reconnaissance battalion from the 26th Panzer Division, elements of the 1st Fallschirmjäger Division and more. There were regiments of the Hermann Göring Panzer Division and the 15th Panzergrenadier Division, which arrived in the vicinity of Anzio by 23 January 1944. At the same time, General Kesselring ordered General Maximilian Ritter von Pohl, in charge of Rome's anti-aircraft guns, to send as many 88mm guns as possible to the Anzio beachhead. The intention was to send them to set up an anti-tank screen to the south of the Italian capital.

Once the US 5th Army had failed to exploit their initial success in landing thousands of troops at Anzio it now appeared that it was down to the Germans to try to expel them from their 6-mile deep bridgehead. On 7 February, the first of many German counter-attacks was launched, but failed to make much headway.

The attack was aimed at the British 1st Division and US VI Corps in the direction of the Allied salient around Carroceto and Aprilia. Fighting continued the next day but the 1st Division under the command of General Penney held its positions despite heavy German pressure. On the 9th the German attacks by the 76th Panzer Corps and the 1st Parachute Corps succeeded in taking both Carroceto and Aprilia. On 16 February, the 14th Army began a massive attack against Anzio, pushing the Allied troops back to positions they had held since 29 January. On the night of 18/19 February, Allied air raids and artillery bombardments slowed down the German offensive. Heavy German losses and strong resistance by the British 1st Division turned the battles around Anzio into a bloody stalemate with the Germans suffering 3,500 casualties, which meant that their attack had to be suspended. A message from General Westphal, the German chief of staff, admitted that the strong Allied resistance and heavy bombing from the air and from the Allied navies meant that his men could not 'throw them back into the sea'. Despite the lack of success and exhaustion of their troops, the Germans launched what turned into another largely futile offensive against Anzio on the 28th. Heavy rain badly affected the attack and German tanks were reported to be sinking in the mud, while their artillery was ineffective due to poor visibility. A final attack on 3 March was contained by the US 3rd Division, ending the fighting around Anzio for several months. During the various German attacks against the Anzio beachhead, the build-up of Allied strength reached 90,000 US and 35,000 British troops. On the Allied side, the mere presence of over 120,000 troops at the German back was seen as a sufficient advantage until the situation was to change. An important move in the Allied ranks saw the replacement of General Lucas as commander of the US 6th Corps by General Lucius Truscott. After several months of inactivity around Anzio, it was time for the troops there to join the fighting against the Gustav Line. General Alexander had decided that the breakout from the Anzio bridgehead should be launched to coincide with the major offensive against the Gustav Line. On 23 May, General Truscott and his two divisions of the US 6th Corps advanced out of the bridgehead. They moved against the German-held town of Cisterna to the north of Anzio, which they took on the 25th, after two days of fighting. The 6th Corps now linked up with US soldiers of the 2nd Corps, who had captured the town of Terracina. As more units marched out of Anzio, they joined the major force now moving towards the Gustav Line.

The Anzio bridgehead had been a costly exercise for the Allies but had also had a major effect on the German war effort in Italy, tying down four of their divisions for months. The battle for Anzio resulted in heavy losses for the German Army, with the 71st and 94th Infantry divisions being destroyed as viable formations. In addition, the 1st Parachute Division, the 90th Panzergrenadier Division and 15th Panzergrenadier Divisions had lost the majority of their effectives. Similar losses had been suffered by the 29th Panzergrenadiers; 715th and 362nd Infantry divisions had also lost most of their men. Also, the 26th Panzer Division had lost most of its armoured vehicles and the 44th Division had lost the 305th, 131st and 576th regiments from its strength.

The USS *Biscayne*, a US Navy seaplane tender acted as the flagship for the amphibious landing at Anzio on 22 January 1944. She had served during the Allied landing at Salerno on 9 September 1943 and then became the flagship of Rear Admiral F.J. Lowry. She is pictured off the coast of Italy in the hours before the landings at Anzio, ready to use her 130mm guns in support. (*US Navy Archives*)

This US Navy photograph shows a Luftwaffe plane being shot down during the first day of the Allied landings at Anzio on 22 January. Operation Shingle involved two headquarters ships, two submarines, four cruisers, twenty-eight destroyers, 103 smaller warships and 241 landing ships and landing craft. Once the German Navy's minefield had been cleared, the landings went surprisingly smoothly despite the attention of the Luftwaffe. (*US Navy Archives*)

A German bomb lands close to the Anzio invasion fleet on the first day of landings on the west coast of Italy in Operation Shingle. Luftwaffe bombing was half-hearted and the vast majority of ships taking part in the invasion were undamaged. On land, the Allied troops landed to little or no resistance as the German commander had decided to end the permanent stand-to that had been in force. The assault on the Gustav Line had distracted the Germans from the invasion to their north and few troops were available to resist the initial landing. (*US Navy Archives*)

US troops come ashore near the town of Nettuno, which along with Anzio was the initial objective of the Allied landings on 22 January. German opposition to the landings was not well co-ordinated at first but reinforcements were soon sent to try to stop any expansion of the Allied bridgehead. By 25 January, Allied advances to the north-west and north-east had taken a few villages and the bridgehead was fairly secure. (*Author's Collection*)

A group of German soldiers are brought into Allied lines around Nettuno in the early stages of the landings around Anzio. The lack of resistance to the initial landings may have lulled the US and British troops into a false sense of security. However, there were many officers and troops who had faced the German Army in North Africa and Sicily who knew that the Germans would strike back at the bridgehead in strength. These Germans appear to be from an administrative unit rather than frontline troops, with one man carrying a suitcase into captivity. (*Author's Collection*)

German paratroopers are rushed by road to try to stem any Allied consolidation of the Anzio bridgehead in January 1944. They belong to the 1st Fallschirmjäger Division, elements of which were sent to the bridgehead along with other units from all over Italy. The German high command in Italy was determined to crush the Allied forces at Anzio before they had the chance to advance northwards. (*Author's Collection*)

Heavily armed soldiers of the Hermann Göring Fallschirm-Panzer Division march towards the Anzio bridgehead on 17 February 1944. They are travelling southwards from their temporary HQ at Cisterna and are passing a disabled Elefant heavy tank destroyer. The Elefant, produced in limited numbers from 1943, was armed with the dreaded 88mm Panzerjägerkanone anti-tank gun and proved to be an effective weapon; it equipped the 1st Company, 653rd Heavy Panzerjäger Battalion on the Anzio–Nettuno front. In total, the Germans had eleven of these brand-new tank destroyers available. This Elefant has been put out of action temporarily by an Allied mine. (*NAC*)

The Barbarigo Battalion of the 'X MAS' – 'Decima Mas' – are marching through Rome on their way to fight alongside the German Army at Anzio. This independent unit of the Italian National Republican Army (ENR) was regarded by the Germans as one of the more reliable Italian Fascist units. Most German officers thought that the elite units of the ENR had fighting qualities that most of the pre-1943 Army didn't have. It could be assumed that anyone who volunteered to serve in the ENR still had loyalty to Benito Mussolini. (*Rudy D'Angelo*)

The 508th Heavy Panzer Battalion was formed in France in May 1943 using personnel from the 29th Panzer Regiment and was under the command of Major Hudel. It had an operational strength of forty-five tanks and was to be sent to Italy seven months later in an effort to reinforce the German and Italian forces pinning the Allied armies in the Anzio beachhead in early 1944. (*Cody Images*)

A Tiger V tank of the 508th Heavy Panzer Battalion, which had a long operational history in Italy in 1944 and 1945, is driving through Rome in February 1944. The battalion fought at Anzio and this tank is on its way southwards to oppose the Allied beachhead. Although the tanks of the 508th had been transported by rail, they had to be unloaded at Ficulle and driven the remaining distance via Rome. (*Author's Collection*)

These 400 US Army Rangers have been taken prisoner during an unsuccessful raid on the town of Cisterna, to the north of Anzio, in late January 1944. They had been captured during the fighting on 30 January and transported northwards to be paraded in front of the citizens of the Italian capital in early February. Nazi propaganda always wanted to use any opportunity to show the German people that the war was going well in Italy. (*Author's Collection*)

The crew of the famous 'Anzio Annie' rail gun are ready to put a 560lb shell into its breech to begin the bombardment of the Allied bridgehead. There were eight of these guns, known as 28cm Kanone 5, in German service during the Second World War, with two nicknamed 'Robert' and 'Leopold' shipped to Italy in early 1944. During the fighting in Italy, the two guns were renamed, with the second gun becoming the 'Anzio Express' because of the noise it made when fired. Both superguns were 94 feet long with a range of 38 miles and were mounted on a huge carriage that allowed them to be towed into position. (*NAC*)

Field Marshal Albert Kesselring is pictured on a tour of German defensive positions around Anzio with his ADC. Kesselring (1885–1960) was made chief of staff of the Luftwaffe and organised the German Air Force during the Polish 1939 and France 1940 campaigns. He was promoted to the highest rank of field marshal in 1940 and commanded the Luftwaffe during the North African Campaign. His ability to develop good relations with Italian commanders made him the obvious choice to be given command in Italy from 1943. After a serious car accident and surgery, he returned to the Italian Front in January 1945 but was then sent to France, where he served from late March to May 1945. (*Author's Collection*)

US Army Major General Lucian Truscott looks at a map of the Anzio region from his field headquarters at Nettuno. He was a colonel in 1942 and was largely responsible for the formation of US special forces based on the British Commandos. During 1942 he was promoted to the rank of major general and commanded troops in Morocco during Operation Torch. In March 1943, he was given command of the 3rd Infantry Division and led them during the invasion of Sicily. His division became the best unit in the US 7th Army and he commanded them as they fought on the Italian mainland in 1943. At Anzio, he commanded the 6th Corps after being given command of the formation in February 1944. He replaced General John. P. Lucas, who had failed to expand the Anzio bridgehead in the first days of the fighting. Lucas explained that he believed the forces at his disposal were too weak to support a breakout. (*Author's Collection*)

A young Fallschirmjäger machine-gunner looks nervously to the skies as he and his comrades move up to their forward positions at Nettuno in early 1944. On the left side of his M38 paratrooper helmet, he has a winged eagle holding swastika decal while on the other side would be a black, white and red shield. He is armed with the MG42 Mauser general-purpose machine gun, which entered service in 1942 and was the best machine gun in German use. In preparation for his guard duty, the paratrooper has an army issue blanket over his shoulder. *(NAC)*

During the fighting around Anzio and Nettuno, the Germans launched a number of fierce counter-attacks. The first assault on the British defence lines began on 3 February, causing 1,400 casualties in the British 1st Division. Another German attack was launched on the 5th against US troops of the 3rd Division and went on for several days, with heavy losses on both sides. In mid-February, on the 15th at 6.00 am, another major German offensive against the Anzio bridgehead began. This attack nearly broke the Allied lines but ended on the 19th with 3,500 German troops being killed on the final day of the offensive. Here a German Luftwaffe ground unit is preparing to move forward against Allied lines, with the support of a Flak 18 20mm anti-aircraft gun being used against ground troops. (*NAC*)

German 88mm anti-aircraft guns are dug in close to the Anzio bridgehead in early 1944 in an attempt to deal with Allied aircraft supporting the Allies. The Germans were determined that any advance by the Allies out of their bridgehead would be fought with all available forces. Air support was vital to the Allied armies during the decisive fighting around Anzio in January and February as aggressive German counteroffensives were launched against the port. In May, the fourteen batteries of 88mms had to be deployed as anti-tank guns as Kesselring had no other guns available to counter the Allied attacks. (*Author's Collection*)

Above: German paratroopers wade across a river close to Aprilia village to the north of Anzio, which was fought over in January and February 1944. These men belong to the 1st Fallschirmjäger Division, which had been rushed to the Anzio region in January to try to deal with the Allied landings there. In early February, the Germans succeeded in taking the village but failed to take the British strongpoint known as 'The Factory'. After the Germans were forced to retire, a US war correspondent said: 'There were dead bodies everywhere, I have never seen so many dead men in one place. They lay so close I had to step with care.' *(NAC)*

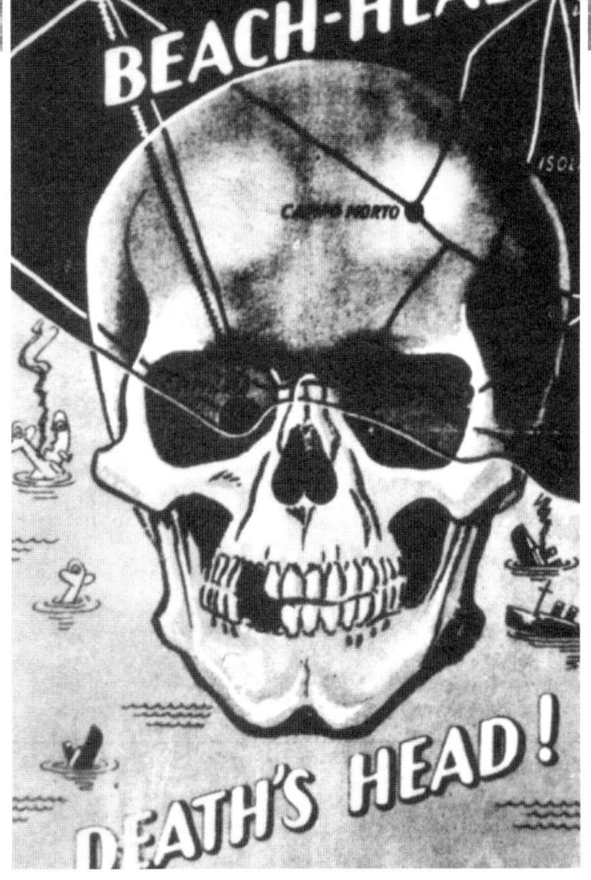

Right: This German propaganda leaflet was dropped over Allied lines during the fighting around Anzio in an attempt to demoralise their troops. However, the growing casualty rate on both sides during the Anzio Campaign did affect both Axis and Allied morale. The play on words of 'Beach-Head, Death's Head!' and the graphics around the skull were intended to force the Allied troops to see the stark reality of their situation. *(Author's Collection)*

Happy British troops move up from the bridgehead at Anzio to fight the German forces trying desperately to stop any Allied advance. German counter-attacks had been ongoing since January with mixed results and both sides had sustained heavy casualties. Entire German formations had virtually been destroyed during the January offensives and the fighting for Anzio and Nettuno turned into a bloody stalemate. These soldiers carry their kit and weapons with them and are dressed for the coming fighting. They wear a variety of uniform items and each soldier prepares himself for the conditions that he will face in the trenches and gun positions at the front. (*Author's Collection*)

Two grenadiers from a Panzergrenadier division look exhausted but determined during the heavy fighting around Anzio in early 1944. During the January battle around the towns of Anzio and Nettuno, elements of the 3rd and 15th Panzergrenadier divisions were heavily involved. The man on the left of the photograph has been issued with an Italian Beretta MP38 sub-machine gun. (*NAC*)

During the fighting for Anzio, paratroopers of the 4th Fallschirmjäger Division fought alongside Italian paratroopers of the 'Nembo' Autonomous Parachute Battalion. Here German paratroopers are in conversation with an Italian paratrooper armed with a Beretta M1938A sub-machine gun slung on his back. Some elite Italian pro-Fascist units like the Nembo were well regarded by their German allies, unlike the bulk of the Italian Army. (*Author's Collection*)

Paratroopers of the 'Nembo' Autonomous Parachute Battalion gather around to discuss their next mission in support of the German Army at the town of Nettuno in the spring of 1944. Small units of Italian pro-Fascist troops were volunteering to serve alongside the Germans from the first days of the fighting on mainland Italy. Most of the officers in this photograph are wearing the Italian paratroopers' camouflaged smock along with the Model 1942 helmet. (*NAC*)

German paratroopers of the 4th Division take a water break during the fighting around the Anzio bridgehead in the spring of 1944. These elite airborne troops had good morale and the relationship between officers and their men was usually superb. After the disaster of Crete in 1941, when the airborne losses during the landings were extremely heavy, paratroopers spent the rest of the war fighting as ground troops. (*NAC*)

German armoured vehicles gather at an assembly point in the Nettuno region close to the Anzio battlefront. On the right of the photograph, the Tiger Pz. Kpfw VI Model E heavy tank has been covered with foliage by its crew. As well as dealing with the increasing Allied ground forces, the Germany Army in Italy had to deal with constant Allied air attacks. The Tiger's 88mm main armament was to prove potent right until the end of the war, but they were eventually defeated by lack of numbers. (*NAC*)

German paratroopers use the cover of a mountain stream to move up to their forward positions during the battle for Anzio. The 1st Fallschirmjäger Division had a major role in holding the defence lines around Anzio from January to June 1944. These paratroopers are carrying all their equipment with them, as they could not rely on regular supplies, largely due to the difficulty of the terrain. (*NAC*)

A 170mm Kanone 18 heavy artillery piece is just about to fire a shell towards the Allied bridgehead at Anzio in early 1944. Several of the crewmen are covering their ears to protect them from the blast of the gun, which could fire up to 17 miles. With a well-drilled crew, the Kanone 18 could fire up to two rounds a minute, and these guns laid down a heavy bombardment during the fighting for Anzio. The Kanone 18 had entered service with the Germans in 1941 and became the most dominant heavy artillery piece of its kind in Wehrmacht service. (*NAC*)

A pair of 105mm Howitzer Motor Carriage M7 self-propelled guns move up a slope on the outskirts of the Anzio bridgehead to try to push the Germans back. This armoured vehicle was armed with the standard 105mm howitzer and was one of the most useful self-propelled guns used by the US Army. It was first used in action in North Africa with the British 8th Army in the Battle of El Alamein, when ninety were employed. In Italy, the M7 was known in the British Army as the 'Priest' due to its pulpit-shaped machine-gun mount. Although welcomed into British service during the Italian Campaign, there were supply problems with the 105mm ammunition, which was not in common use with the 8th Army. (*US Army Archives*)

German soldiers of a Luftwaffe Field Division dig into the hillside after arriving from the north to secure the Anzio bridgehead and stop the breakout of Allied troops. During the Italian Campaign, the Germans received reinforcement from several Luftwaffe field divisions. These were formed from surplus Luftwaffe personnel and were sent as infantry, mostly to the Russian front. Training of the Luftwaffe field divisions was not quite up to the standard of their army comrades and many were loath to serve in the formations. The two Luftwaffe field divisions in Italy were the 19th and 20th, which were deployed there in June and May 1944 respectively. While the 19th was sent into defensive positions at Livorno, the 20th was used in a coastal protection and anti-partisan role. (*NAC*)

The German Army moved large numbers of tanks and other armoured vehicles to the Nettuno sector near Anzio, including this Sturmpanzer IV 'Brummbär', or 'Growling Bear'. It was produced in small numbers by the Vomag factory and was based on the Panzer IV chassis. Armed with the 15cm Sturmhaubitze L/12, the Brummbär first saw action during the Battle of Kursk on the Russian front in 1943. Only 313 of these Stu.Pz. 43s were built during the war. Production of small numbers of numerous varieties of armoured vehicles by the Germans proved disastrous. Meanwhile, the Soviets and Allies standardised their production to a few models of tanks and other armoured vehicles. (*NAC*)

A column of British prisoners march past two German armoured vehicles during the fighting for the Anzio bridgehead in March 1944. The larger vehicle is a Sturmpanzer IV 'Brummbär', or 'Growling Bear', while the smaller vehicle is a Panzerkampfwagen II light tank. Panzer IIs were designed as a stopgap until larger tanks could be designed and produced. Most had been taken out of service by 1944, but some were still used in Italy and the Balkans, as is evidenced here. (*NAC*)

A US Sherman M4 tank of the 5th Army is unloaded from USS *LST-177* on the waterfront of the port of Anzio on 27 April 1944. During the fighting around Anzio and the town of Nettuno, there were times when the Allies could literally have been pushed back into the sea. The timely arrival of reinforcements could swing the balance back in the favour of the Allied forces. (*US National Archives*)

A US PACK 75mm howitzer fires from its camouflaged position in the Anzio bridgehead to German lines. During the battle for the bridgehead, the Allies were firing an average of 25,000 rounds per day. As the fighting progressed, the number of artillery pieces available to the Allied force increased steadily, with heavier artillery arriving in March and April. (*US Army Archives*)

This group of German soldiers were taken prisoner during the fighting for the Anzio bridgehead in April. The American guard looks relaxed as his captives appear to have had all the fight taken out of them. By early April, a good deal of the fighting around the beachhead consisted of artillery duels, with the Allies having an upper hand as more and more guns were concentrated. These men are bound for a temporary prisoner of war camp somewhere within the beachhead. (*Author's Collection*)

Chapter Eight

June-August 1944 Into Central Italy

After the Germans evacuated Rome on 4 June 1944, the German 14th Army began a retreat northwards along roads clogged with vehicles. The main objective for the Allied armies following their liberation of Rome was to cut off the withdrawing German 10th and 14th armies. It was hoped to stop the two German armies from joining and forming a united defence of the Gothic Line to the north. The US 5th Army was to advance to the Arno River and the three cities Pisa–Lucca–Pistoia while the 8th Army was to aim for Florence–Arezzo–Bibbiena, along a 200-mile front. The US 5th Army had three mechanised and eight infantry divisions and were instructed to make a thrust towards the junction of the 10th and 14th armies. They were told not to worry about protecting their flanks and were to move forward towards their objectives in order to push into the Arno Valley and break the German defences on the Apennine Line from Florence to Bologna. In order to release engineering equipment including pontoon bridges and transport vehicles, the offensive up the Adriatic coast was suspended. Kesselring was pleasantly surprised by the concentrated offensive by the US 5th Army as he feared an advance on a broad front. He believed that an offensive on a broad front would have probably seen the disintegration of the 14th Army. Facing the rather slow US 5th Army advance were the 29th and 90th Panzergrenadier divisions and the 26th Panzer Division. They had taken positions along the Tiber River crossing between Rome and Orvieto, where they delayed the Allied advance. German delaying actions were important as they allowed the completion of the Gothic Line defences that were so vital to stopping the Allied advance.

Both sides were making some logistical changes as the Allied advance from Rome began in early June. The US IV Corps replaced the VI Corps on 9 June and were joined by the French Expeditionary Corps (FEC), who were soon to be transferred for their part in the invasion of southern France – Operation Dragoon. French Expeditionary Corps units now spent their final days in Italy attacking the Albert Line, whose temporary defences were intended to protect the Gothic Line. Behind the protection of the Albert Line, the German 10th and 14th armies were being reorganised into a unified Army Group 'C'.

On 6 June, the 6th South African Armoured Division crossed the Aniene River and captured Civita Castellana. This advance was countered by the arrival of the German 356th Infantry Division and the 162nd Turkoman Division, manned by former Soviet POWs. At the same time along the Tyrrhenian coast, the US 34th Division captured Civitavecchia, to the north of Rome. Again the Germans countered by bringing forward an armoured division and the 90th Panzergrenadier Division to the south-west of the town of Orvieto. The 6th South African still managed to cross the Tiber River and take Orvieto on 14 June. While the

5th Army was struggling forward, their counterparts in the 8th Army were also trying to push northwards. They were under Alexander's orders from 7 June to attack north-west through the Umbria region and head towards the city of Bologna on the Arno River. Despite German rearguard actions, the 8th Army managed to advance 100 miles behind the retreating enemy. Hopes that the Allied advance would be able to push through the Gothic Line and then into northern Italy were looking optimistic. As the 8th Army advance stalled, the US 5th Army was still moving up the Tyrrhenian coast, with Cecina being captured on 2 July. This success was followed by the taking of the port of Livorno – 'Leghorn' – on the 19th and the city of Pisa on 23 July. The newly arrived US 91st Division reached Pontedera on the Arno River on the same day. They were joined along the Arno by the US 88th Division, and the 5th Army was poised to move against Florence.

Since 7 June, on the 8th Army's left flank the XIII Corps had been advancing and had successfully crossed the Tiber River. Its 8th Indian Division captured Spoleto and Trevi in mid-June and advanced towards the city of Perugia. Their advance was blocked by the German 76th Panzer Corps manning the Albert Line and had to wait for the bulk of 13th Corps to move up to the front. On 20 June, the British 4th and 78th Infantry divisions, the 6th South African Armoured Division and the Canadian 1st Armoured Brigade of 13th Corps attacked the Albert Line. It took eight days to break the German defences, with the defenders withdrawing as usual to fight another day. Meanwhile on the Adriatic coast, the stalled June offensive was restarted led by the Polish II Corps, which returned to the front line after resting after hard fighting at Cassino. The Poles went straight on to the offensive and took Ancona after some hard fighting on 18 July. The XIII Corp's next objective was the rail hub at Arezzo, which would be a vital supply base for the 8th Army and was taken on 18 July. For the assault, the 8th and 10th Indian divisions and 2nd New Zealand Division were added to the 13th's strength. They faced a German scratch force made up of units from the 334th and 715th Infantry divisions, 1st Parachute and 15th Panzergrenadier Division. As the British XIII Corps were advancing, they were joined by the 10th Corps and then the V Corps. By 22 August, the 8th Army on the Adriatic coast had also reached the Metauro River just to the south of the Gothic Line. On the left flank of the front, the 5th Army, the 8th Army in the centre and the Polish II Corps were on the Adriatic coast.

The various Allied armies had begun to converge on Florence from 22 July and the German garrison prepared to withdraw, with Kesselring declaring it an 'open city'. By 2 August, the Germans had crossed to the north bank of the Arno River, blowing up most of the bridges over it. On 4 August, the 8th and 10th Indian divisions and the 2nd New Zealand Division had reached the southern bank of the river. At the same time, the South African 6th Armoured Division was advancing into the suburbs of the city. German defenders were reduced in number and were almost totally lacking in armour and artillery. Florence fell on the 11th, and by 22 August, the Allies were poised a few miles south of the much-vaunted Gothic Line. After Florence was captured, Alexander wanted to continue the 8th Army's advance to penetrate the Gothic Line and advance on their major objective, Bologna. However, both the US 5th and 8th armies needed to reorganise and refit before any further advance. Over the previous few months, the US 5th Army had suffered 18,000 casualties while the 8th Army had lost 16,000 men. The Germans were equally unprepared for any more fighting, having lost a staggering 63,000 killed, wounded or missing. Although the Allied respite was vital to their continued war effectiveness, the lull did allow the Germans also to recover. In addition, it allowed the Germans to finish more of the Gothic Line, which was soon to face a major attack from late August.

US General Mark Clark, commander of the US 5th Army, arrives at the front to celebrate the meeting of his troops with those breaking out of the Anzio beachhead. On 25 May, forward patrols from Anzio made contact with US 5th Army units in a highly symbolic moment for the Allied cause in Italy. It was now possible for the Allies to push forward towards the next German defensive lines in the north. (*Author's Collection*)

Two American soldiers look over a disabled Hummel Sd.Kfz. 165 self-propelled gun on the outskirts of Cisterna on 27 May 1944. The Hummel had a 150mm gun and had been produced from early 1943, and usually operated in heavy self-propelled artillery batteries with six guns and one tracked ammunition carrier. The 5th Army had been fighting for the town to the north of Anzio since January and it finally fell at the end of May. In late May, when the breakout from the Anzio beachhead began, Cisterna was the first objective for the Americans. (*US Army Archives*)

One of the first casualties of the fighting for the strategic town of Cisterna in late May is carried to the rear by his comrades. The attack on Cisterna from the south began on 23 May and was led by the US 135th Regiment of the 34th Division. In support of the infantry advance was the 1st Armoured Division with its Sherman M4 medium tanks. The attack was also supported by the British 1st and 5th Infantry divisions, who made a diversionary attack on the Germans on the 22nd. (*US Army Archives*)

German soldiers with their arms held aloft rush across no man's land to surrender to the US troops who have taken the town of Cisterna in late May 1944. The youth of some of these soldiers indicates that the stretched German Army was having to conscript younger and younger men by mid-1944. The German defenders included units of the 1st Parachute Division, the 955th Infantry Regiment and some units of the 715th Infantry Division. These units had been reinforced by the 1028th Panzergrenadier Division. *(Author's Collection)*

Below: Sherman M4 tanks of the 13th Armoured Regiment move into the outskirts of Rome on 4 June. At this time there were still German troops strongly resisting in the Alban Hills to the south-west of the city. Later in the day, the US 88th Division entered the famous Piazza Venezia in the centre of Rome. *(Author's Collection)*

American troops of the 88th Division chat to citizens of Rome on the day they entered the Italian capital, where they were mostly welcomed by the population. These Italian women are greeting the US troops with some freshly made food, which seems to be gratefully received. In general, the Italian people were happy to be rid of their Fascist government and the German occupiers. (*US Army Archives*)

General Sir Oliver Leese, the commander-in-chief of the 8th Army, discusses the progress of the campaign in central Italy with Allied Commander-in-Chief General Sir Harold Alexander. Leese had replaced Montgomery in December 1943 and continued in this command until he was sent to serve in Southeast Asia in September 1944. He was recognised for his service during the Italian Campaign, being given a knighthood in the field by King George on 26 July 1944. *(Author's Collection)*

A platoon of Indian troops march into the town of Terni, which fell to the 8th Army on 14 June 1944. Terni, which is 65 miles north of Rome, came under Allied pressure from the British XIII Corps from early June. The city had come under heavy bombing by the Allies due to the war industries that were based there. The 8th Indian Division, which these soldiers belong to, had the support of the 1st Canadian Armoured Brigade. *(Author's Collection)*

A Sherman M4 medium tank crosses a Bailey bridge, which has just been built by a field company of the Royal Engineers. The bridge, close to the town of Orvieto, had been built to replace the original one blown up by the retreating Germans. Riding on the tank are the personnel from the unit's artillery observation team being given a lift to their new position. Orvieto fell to the Allies on 14 June, leaving the approaches to the Gothic Line within striking distance. (*Author's Collection*)

An M4 Sherman medium tank of 11th Brigade approaches the town of Orvieto, whose people were spared the destruction seen in other similar towns. As they approached the town on 14 June and prepared to open fire, a young German officer drove towards them in a Volkswagen car holding a large white flag. British troops had fully expected to have to fight for the town as other towns and villages had been turned into fortifications by the Germans, but Orvieto was spared when a surrender was agreed. *(Author's Collection)*

Another Italian town falls to the 8th Army in June 1944 and three of its liberators have found a swastika flag to display as a war trophy. During June, the 8th Army had advanced northwards along with the 5th Army, their main objective being the Gothic Line. All the men have their hands on the prized German flag, and it may have to be played for by a game of cards. *(Author's Collection)*

A Canadian infantryman checks out a Panther tank turret that has been dug into a hidden defensive position covered in foliage in early June 1944. Most of these surplus turrets were placed in concrete emplacements in hilltop positions but this one appears to be situated in open ground. The turrets were adapted for use as pillboxes by having extra armour added to their top, from 16mm to 40mm. By February 1944, 112 of these turrets had been built, followed by a second batch of 155 by August 1944. These turret emplacements were often difficult to spot by the advancing Allies and might destroy a number of tanks and other targets before being dealt with. Of course, once their positions were located they were sitting ducks for Allied artillery fire. (*Author's Collection*)

A British soldier shelters under the wreck of a Mark VI Tiger heavy tank while having a cigarette. Although he would probably be safe smoking in the open, there was always the possibility of a German sniper bullet. The Tiger tank has been disabled by an Allied air attack and has been pushed off the road by Allied Engineers. According to the original caption for the photograph, such 'shelters' were dotted along the line of the Allied advance. (*Author's Collection*)

The crew of a 75mm Pak 40 have sited their gun at the top of a hill in central Italy to dominate the valley below in mid-June. Although they have positioned the gun under the cover of an olive tree, they are still exposed to air attack from the dominant Allied air forces in 1944. (*Author's Collection*)

Above: British troops move cautiously through the rubble-strewn streets of an Italian town on the lookout for remaining German defenders, including snipers. They are entering the town of Castiglione, in the Lake Trasimeno area, in late June, and are using any available cover as they move forward. Castiglione, which fell on 26 June, is a mountain town about 40 miles from the city of Bologna. (*Author's Collection*)

Right: In the early morning light, a German soldier moves along a path keeping as low a profile as possible. When this photograph was taken, the German Army was withdrawing most of its best troops to the Gothic Line. The Germans had evacuated Florence on 11 August after destroying nearly all of the bridges over the Arno River, which runs through the city. (*Author's Collection*)

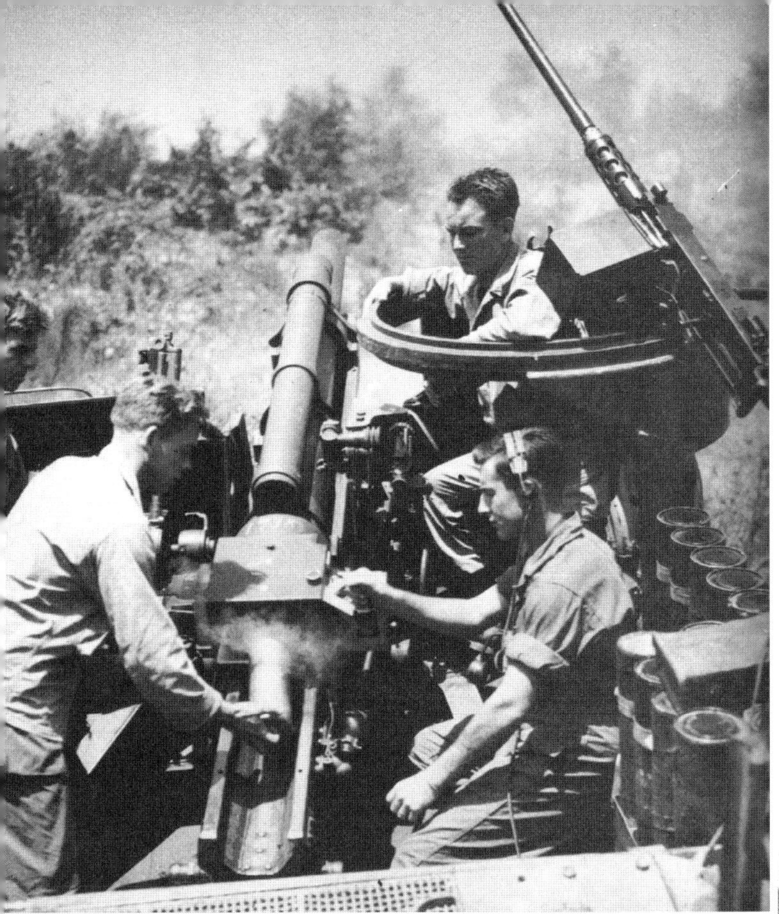

In a lull in fighting during July, this US 5th Army crew of an M7 Priest self-propelled gun take part in gun training on their 105mm howitzer on the west bank of the Arno River. The 5th Army had arrived on the bank of the Arno on 18 July and by the beginning of August were grouped along a 35-mile front. *(Author's Collection)*

Soldiers of the 3rd Battalion the Welsh Guards march towards Florence in early August, having taken part in the battle for Monte Cassino a few months before. The dominance of mountainous warfare during the Italian Campaign is evidenced by the roll call of the 3rd Battalion's battle honours. Besides their fight at Cassino, they took part in five battles for German-held mountains: Monte Purgatorio, Monte Grande, Monte Piccolo, Monte Battaglia, Monte Verro. *(Author's Collection)*

A left-wing partisan is seen in Florence on 14 August 1944 posing for the Allied news cameraman. He has armed himself with an ex-Italian Army Carcano Moschetto 91 carbine and has been able to gather a reasonable number of bullets for it. Italian soldiers who were unemployed after the German takeover were often forced into working as labourers for the occupiers. Many went into the hills to fight the Germans rather than suffer the privations and indignities of being a forced worker for the enemy. During the liberation of Florence on 11 August, Italian sources claimed that the resistance in the city had suffered 5,000 dead and 8,000 missing. (*Author's Collection*)

Below: South African troops move cautiously forward through the streets of Florence on 11 August. The city had effectively fallen to Italian resistance forces after the Germans had withdrawn from the city on 7 August. As they prepared to retire from Florence, the Germans had destroyed all but one bridge over the Arno River in late July. The only bridge spared, on the orders of the German commander Gerhard Wolf, was the world-famous Ponte Vecchio. For this decision, Wolf was later given recognition by the Italians. (*Author's Collection*)

Chapter Nine

1943-45
The Air War Over Italy

When the fighting began in Sicily in July 1943, the Allied air power in the Mediterranean stood at 104 squadrons of fighters and ninety-five squadrons of bombers. There were also twenty-nine squadrons of transport planes and forty-three squadrons of reconnaissance, torpedo bombers and maritime patrol aircraft. At that time, the available Allied aircraft totalled approximately 4,000. They were faced by the Luftwaffe Luftflotte II under Generalfeldmarschall Wolfram von Richthofen and a number of Regia Aeronautica aircraft. At the start of the Sicilian Campaign, the combined Axis air power based in Sardinia, Sicily and southern Italy was between 1,500 and 1,600 aircraft. Allied forces seized a number of airfields on Sicily, from where their planes were soon operating. These captured airfields gave the RAF, SAAF and USAF a great advantage as heavy Allied bombing of southern Italy meant that Axis aircraft had to fly from bases in Sardinia and central Italy. By 21 July, the Axis air forces had lost 216 aircraft, with the Allies losing only eighty-seven planes. They reportedly had to leave 1,000 of their planes on abandoned airfields as the surviving aircraft continued to fly from airfields on the Italian mainland. Before they left them, the German ground crew destroyed the vast majority of aircraft and any other usable equipment. By the end of the fighting on Sicily, Axis planes were having to fly from central Italy as Allied bombers had destroyed many airfields in the south of the country. In five weeks of fighting, the Luftwaffe and Regia Aeronautica had lost 1,850 aircraft while the Allies had only suffered 400 losses.

By August 1943, the Luftwaffe in Italy had 841 planes, but by the end of the year, there were only 341 available to fly. The following year saw a downward trend, with 370 in January, 566 in March, 125 in July and 104 in November. In the final months of the war in Italy, the Luftwaffe did receive reinforcements, giving it a strength of 217 in March 1945. When the campaign moved to mainland Italy in September 1943, the Luftwaffe soon lost the support of the Regia Aeronautica. Some of its pilots later joined the pro-Allied Aviazione Cobelligerante Italiana (Italian Co-Belligerent Air Force) while their former comrades chose to fly alongside the Germans. The Luftwaffe in Italy was supported by a number of pro-Fascist pilots who flew for the Aeronautica Nazionale Repubblicana. During the air battles of 1944 and early 1945, the ANR shot down 262 Allied planes, losing 158 planes themselves.

Throughout the fighting on mainland Italy, the RAF, USAF and associated air forces had a total superiority over the Luftwaffe. For most of the September 1943 to May 1945 period, the strength of the Allied air forces in the Mediterranean stood at about 4,000 planes. While the Allied air forces had other roles to fulfil, the total number of planes available for service in Italy was always overwhelming. Large-scale campaigns by Allied bombers, especially during 1944, severely affected the German war effort in Italy. When needed, the full weight of the USAF XXII Tactical Air Command and the RAF's Mediterranean Allied Strategic Air Force No. 205 Group could be sent against enemy targets. Before the 8th and US 5th armies attacked one of the many German defensive lines during their advance up Italy, they would be softened up by raids involving several hundred bombers. The largest raid in Italy took place over Milan on the night of 13/14 August 1943, when 1,900 bombs were dropped.

An advance party of the RAF landed at the abandoned air base at Montecorvino and found a single Luftwaffe Fw 190 fighter. The German plane was being prepared to go on a fighter-bomber mission when the Axis forces withdrew from the airfield. During the fighting in Sicily, the handful of Fw 190s based on the island were faced by a far superior number of RAF and USAF fighters. By 18 July, there were reportedly only twenty-five serviceable Luftwaffe aircraft on the island. (*Author's Collection*)

Most Sicilian airfields were speedily captured by British and US forces, including RAF units that landed at abandoned German bases. These RAF pilots sitting on the wing of a captured Me 109 fighter belong to the 43rd Squadron, which had fought in North Africa. The squadron, which had fought during the Battle of Britain in 1940, proudly carried the nickname 'Fighting Cocks'. They are posing for a photograph while waiting to be sent on another sortie over the skies of Sicily, which were increasingly controlled by the Allies. *(Author's Collection)*

These bomb-shaped petrol containers are being unloaded from a German Ju 52 transport plane in southern Italy. As soon as Allied troops landed at several points in the south, the German Armed Forces reacted. Tanks, artillery and other heavy weaponry was rushed from northern Italy southwards. Of course, the petrol needed to feed the German war machine was moved towards the battlefront to keep their vehicles on the road. *(Author's Collection)*

Above: Two RAF Supermarine Spitfire Mk IX fighters of 241 Squadron fly a reconnaissance mission over the Anzio bridgehead on 29 January 1944. They have flown from their base at Madna to the south-east of Campomarino to check the weather over the bridgehead for possible further Allied landings. (*Author's Collection*)

A Royal Air Force Martin Baltimore bomber drops its bombs on the railway station at Sulmona, an important point on the railway running across the Italian peninsula in the spring of 1944. Sulmona is situated to the east of Rome and had strategic value, especially during the defence of the Italian capital. The Baltimore was a light attack-bomber, well protected by up to eight machine guns and could carry 2,000lb of bombs. (*Author's Collection*)

A Royal Air Force Martin B26 Marauder bomber is taking part in a bombing raid on a unnamed Adriatic port. The US bomber had entered service with the RAF in North Africa in 1942 and operated against the Italian coastline and Axis shipping along the Balkan coast. By September 1944, the Marauders in RAF service were taken out of service, largely due to the difficulty of flying the plane, which needed an experienced pilot to handle it. (*Author's Collection*)

A Macchi C205 fighter of the 1st Squadron, 1st Group of the pro-Fascist Aeronautica Nazionale Repubblicana (ANR) is prepared to go on a mission. The 1st Group in July 1944 had a total of twenty-one fighters, with thirteen Macchi C205s and eighteen Fiat G55s in service. These two types of fighter were the best available to the Italian Air Force pre-1943 and were soon taken over by pilots still loyal to Benito Mussolini. (*Author's Collection*)

This Messerschmitt Bf 109G fighter has been supplied to the ANR, the air force of the puppet Italian Air Force, in September 1944 and belongs to the 3rd Squadron of the 11th Fighter Group. The plane has new markings applied, which are a mix of the original German markings with Italian ANR ones. Italian tricolour symbols were carried on the rear fuselage and on the tail of the aircraft, with the plane's individual number in white. (*Private Collection*)

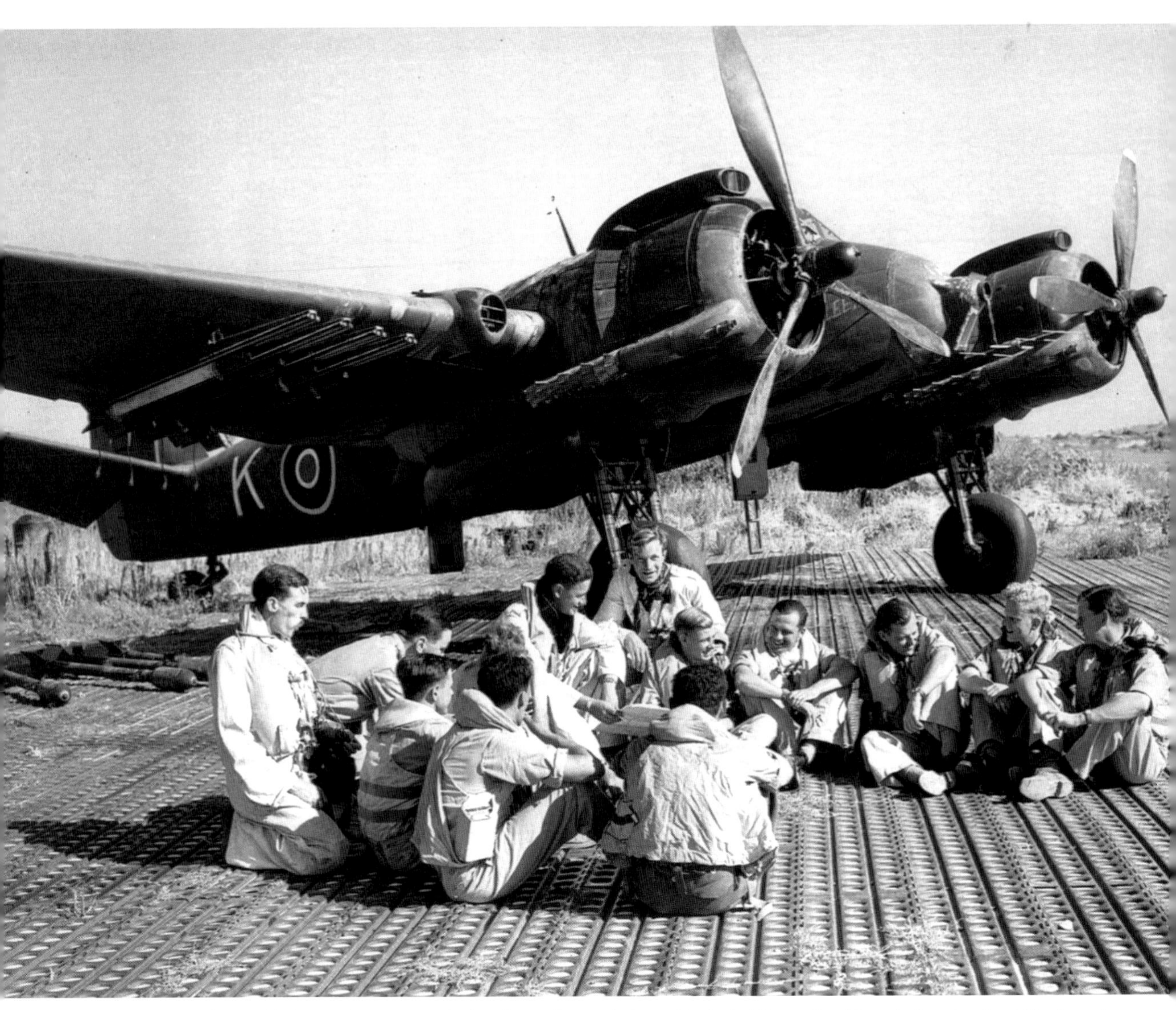

Mixed crews of two Allied squadrons sit on the hard standing and chat with their fellow pilots. They belong to the 16th Squadron of the South African Air Force and the 227th Squadron of the Royal Air Force. Behind them is a Bristol Type 156 Beaufighter strike aircraft, which served in Italy in the ground attack role. Besides with the RAF and the SAAF, the plane also flew with the Canadian and Australian air forces in various theatres of war. They are about to take off from their base close to the Biferno River to a German headquarters at Dubrovnik in Yugoslavia. (*Author's Collection*)

This poor quality photograph features a US-made P-39 Airacobra fighter of the pro-Allied Aviazione Cobelligerante Italiana (ACI, Italian Co-Belligerent Air Force) taxies at its base at Lecce-Galatina. The ACI had four gruppos with two fighter, one bomber and one transport group, which were eventually equipped with US and British aircraft. There were also a number of ex-Italian Air Force aircraft in use, but most of these were obsolete by 1943. ACI aircraft did not fly missions over Italian territory but operated against the Germans in the occupied Balkans. (*Author's Collection*)

US-supplied Martin A-30 Baltimore III light attack-bombers of the pro-Allied ACI fly a bombing mission from their base in southern Italy. The 28th Gruppo Stormo Baltimore was equipped with these modern aircraft to replace a variety of former Italian Air Force planes. Two hundred and eighty-one Italian aircraft had landed at Allied air bases by their pilots who wanted to join the Allies but most were found to be unserviceable. The ACI flew 11,000 missions between 1943 and 1945, largely supporting partisan forces in Yugoslavia and Albania. It was decided that they should not fly missions in Italy so as to avoid clashes between pro-Allied and pro-Fascist pilots. (*Author's Collection*)

Ground crew make a valiant effort to move this Royal Air Force Spitfire fighter from its flooded standing area to a firmer footing. It was the mud of the Italian winter that often held up the Allied offensives in the winters of 1943/44 and 1944/45. The later marks of the famous Spitfire saw widespread service in the skies over Italy and were flown by other Commonwealth countries, including South Africa. Spitfires were also flown in small numbers by the United States Air Force in Italy from 1944. (*Author's Collection*)

These Afro-American aircrew of the 332nd Fighter Group of the USAF are being given a pre-mission briefing at Ramitelli before going into action over northern Italy in March 1945. They were popularly known as the 'Tuskegee Airmen', after the training academy where they received their instruction, the Tuskegee Institute. The first Afro-American unit to see action was the 99th Pursuit Squadron, which flew during the North African and Sicilian campaigns in 1943. Strict US segregation laws made it difficult to train black Americans, as white officers were not supposed to serve in their units. As one US commanding officer said: 'Negro pilots cannot be used in our present Air Corps units since this would result in negro officers serving over white enlisted men.' Regardless of the difficulties, the 332nd Fighter Group, made up of the 100th, 301st and 302nd squadrons, flew missions over Sicily, Anzio, Rome and the Po Valley. They flew P-47 Thunderbolt and P-51 Mustangs, with the latter having the red markings that gave them the alternate nickname 'Red Tails'. (*US Air Force Archives*)

USAF Liberator B-25 medium bombers drop their bombs over Comacchio Lagoon, where German troops are fighting against British commandos in April 1945. The commandos were battling the 162nd Turkistan Division around Lake Comacchio as part of the Allied Spring Offensive. This division had been raised by the desperate Germans from amongst Soviet prisoners of war, who loosely came from the Caucasus region. The commandos launched Operation Roast on 1 April 1945 and were successful in defeating the poor quality and demoralised 162nd Division. (*Author's Collection*)

A Messerschmitt Bf 109G fighter takes off on a mission in April 1945 in one of the last operations by this squadron. As on most fronts, by spring 1945, the Luftwaffe in Italy were heavily outnumbered by the Allied air forces. This particular unit earned its last victory against the Allies on 19 April, when the German armies were on the verge of defeat. (*Private Collection*)

Chapter Ten

August–September 1944 The Gothic Line

With the Gustav Line breached in early June, Field Marshal Kesselring, C-in-C of Army Group C, ordered the 10th and 14th German armies to carry out a fighting withdrawal to the Gothic Line. From the summer of 1943, the German headquarters in Italy identified the importance of building a defence line across the Apennine Mountains in northern Tuscany. The new fallback defence line would protect the Liguria region and ran from the Tyrrhenian Sea near Pisa to the Adriatic coast near Rimini. Initially called the 'Green Line', the substantial defensive line was constructed over a number of months using an estimated 250,000 labourers. They were organised by the German Labour Todt Organisation, with most workers being conscripted Italians, including prisoners of war. At places, concrete emplacements, bunkers and shelters were built to guard strategic passes and roads. In total, the defence line had 479 emplacements for artillery and mortars and at least 2,376 machine-gun nests. Behind the major emplacements were miles of anti-tank ditches and secondary trenches, which were often crudely dug but were protected by 120,000 yards of barbed wire. The Gothic Line was supposed to be protected by a number of dug-in Panther tank turrets but these were not supplied in enough numbers. Fighting for control of the Gothic Line was going to be vital to the situation in Italy and was the last major defence line of the Germans. Before the Allies attacked, Field Marshal Kesselring had assured Hitler that the Gothic Line was impregnable. In reality, the defences had many weaknesses and the western and eastern ends were susceptible to Allied attacks.

When Rome fell in early June, General Alexander had estimated that the Germans would have only ten weak divisions with which to defend the Gothic Line. Hitler had, however, switched seven divisions from various fronts to reinforce Army Group C, which manned the defence line. These divisions came from Denmark, Hungary, the Netherlands, and the Russian front. A battalion of Tiger heavy tanks were sent from France and in addition, three divisions worth of replacements were sent to Italy from German training camps. They were sent to replace the losses suffered by the seasoned divisions that had been decimated in the Liri Valley. Allied plans to take the Gothic Line had been frustrated by the removal of seven of General Alexander's divisions to take part in the invasion of southern France – Operation Dragoon. Alexander had been warned in late May 1944 that he was going to lose these seasoned divisions, including the French Expeditionary Corps, and this was confirmed in early July 1944. Alexander was disappointed by the loss of some of his best units but hoped that the invasion of southern France would serve to distract the Germans in Italy. Although southern France was regarded as being remote from the Italian theatre, a successful invasion could see troops eventually crossing from there into north-west Italy.

The Allied attack on the Gothic Line was planned to begin on 15 August to coincide with the Allied landings in southern France – Operation Dragoon. It was delayed, however, and the first joint assaults by the US 5th and 8th armies began on the night of 25/26 August. Winston Churchill was at the front line when the offensive began, and commented: 'This was the nearest I got to the enemy and the time I heard most bullets in the Second World War.' Taken by surprise by the 8th Army's night attack by the 5th Corps – Canadian 1st Corps and Polish 2nd Corps – the German 76th Armoured Corps put up little resistance. In the early fighting, the Allied troops established a bridgehead when they crossed the Metauro River on the 26th. On 30 August, the British V Corps – Canadian 1st Corps spearheaded by the 46th Division – crossed the Foglia River and attacked the main German defensive position on the other bank. A day later, the Canadians penetrated the Gothic Line defences for the first time but were resisted by the strong German force holding it. The Germans had bulldozed the buildings and trees around their positions, creating killing grounds for their concrete machine-gun nests. Artillery posts had been blasted in the Apennine rock and deep minefields sown from the Adriatic in the east to the Ligurian Sea. Facing the Allied offensive were the 26th Panzer, the 29th Panzergrenadier and the 98th Infantry Division. These formations were joined by the 162nd Turkestan Division, which had been formed in May 1943 from a mixture of Azeris, Armenians and Georgians. The arrival of this poorly trained foreign division showed how desperate the Germans now were for fresh troops.

General Leese, the 8th Army commander, had prepared for his offensive and had moved troops from the west of Italy to attack on the eastern flank of the Apennines. The aim was to cross the Foglia River and break through the newly completed Gothic Line and clear the way for a mass tank attack into the floodplain of the Po Valley. Leese's initial plan was to advance up Route 64 to Bologna from Pistoia, and along Route 65 from Florence through mountainous terrain. General Leese decided that this route would give him little chance to use his forces' total superiority in armour and artillery. Instead, he decided to concentrate the 8th Army advance on the Adriatic coast, with their main objective the coastal town of Rimini. After a slow start against the German defences, the Canadians had managed to take the towns of Passano, San Savino and Riccione after two weeks of fighting. At the same time, the Marano River was crossed and the 4th Indian Division occupied the principality of San Marino. On 13 September, it looked like the 8th Army was going to break through the Gothic Line at the Gemmano and Coriano ridges. The heavens then opened and torrential rain began, which effectively ended the thrust, with Allied tanks and artillery bogged down in the mud. By the time the British could organise themselves, the German commander had plugged the gap with reinforcements. German forces had established strongholds on the summits of the Gemmano and Coriano hills. Strong attacks by the 5th Armoured Division of the Canadian I Corps and the 1st Division of the British V Corps finally took the hills. The few weeks of fighting had cost the 8th Army dearly, with a staggering 14,000 casualties suffered. Once the hills had been taken, it appeared that the major objective of the 8th Army, Rimini, was now open to their advance. However, as the Canadians of the 8th Army moved towards Rimini, the German defence stiffened considerably. All the villages on the road to Rimini had been fortified and hand-to-hand fighting caused heavy casualties. On 20 September, the town of San Lorenzo fell and the following day Rimini itself fell to the Canadians. It had taken four weeks of hard fighting by the Canadians and the Greek 3rd Mountain Brigade to overcome the stiff German resistance around the Italian resort. On 26 September, the 8th Army crossed the Rubicon River and pushed into the Italian northern plains, and were pushing northwards along the eastern flank of the Apennines.

While the 8th Army was advancing on the eastern sector of the Gothic Line, the US 5th Army was advancing in the central sector from 12 September. Their offensive had begun with a diversionary attack by the US II Corp's 34th Division, which advanced up the fortified Futa Pass, which fell on the 17th. At the same time, the 91st Division made another diversionary advance towards the Giogo Pass, with both passes being north of Florence on the main road to the city of Bologna. Depleted German forces struggled to contain these advances and it was left largely up to the 1st Parachute Corps to try to counter them. Giogo Pass fell to the US II Corps on 18 September and the Futa Pass also fell. By 25 September, the relentless Allied offensive was pushing back the struggling troops of the German 10th and 14th armies. Losses amongst General Lemelsen's 14th and Vietinghoff's 10th armies were disastrous: 10th Army had only ninety battalions; only ten of these had more than 400 men on strength, with thirty-eight of them having only 200 men available. Against the depleted German forces the US 5th Army in the west began a major attack, and within a few days succeeded in piercing the Gothic Line. By the 22nd, the 5th had made major advances and the Germans in the western sector had begun to withdraw northwards. There was now only a small strip of the Gothic Line still in the hands of the 10th Army along the Tyrrhenian coastline.

Italian labourers dig a deep bunker on the Gothic Line as the new defensive line is prepared for the expected Allied attack in the summer of 1944. There were a reported 250,000 labourers working on the defences for months, with many of them being pressed into service by the Germans. The job of building the larger fortifications and bunkers in the defence line was given to the German Todt Organisation. Todt was the civil and military engineering organisation of Nazi Germany from 1933 to 1945. Their policy of employing slave labourers was a stain on the organisation and some of its officials were dealt with in post-war trials. *(Author's Collection)*

British soldiers of the 8th Army practise the operation of a new anti-tank weapon, the PIAT or 'Projector Infantry Anti-Tank'. This weapon may look a little primitive but it was formidable, with a 33lb projectile that was capable of penetrating 4 inches of armour plate. (*Author's Collection*)

A German soldier hands out fruit to his comrades that he has gathered into his steel helmet. The happy soldier receiving a peach is taking cover behind a haystack and keeps his MP40 sub-machine gun at the ready. Most frontline troops had scavengers within their units who could be relied on to get extra food from nearby villages or farms. (*NAC*)

An MG 34 machine-gun team fire from a camouflaged position during the fighting along the Gothic Line in August 1944. After the fall of the Gustav Line, German forces were allowed by Allied prevarication to withdraw further north during early summer to the already prepared Gothic Line. During the withdrawal of the Germans, the newly organised Italian partisans constantly harassed them. (*NAC*)

A German truck is pushed up a mountain road in central Italy with the assistance of Italian prisoners of war. They are being organised by Germans of the National Socialist Motor Corps (Nationalsozialistisches Kraftfahrkorps, NSKK), which was a paramilitary organisation. During the war, its personnel were used to help organise the transport system of the German Army. Most able-bodied men of the NSKK had been drafted into the regular army so it was usually the older and unfit who continued to serve in the organisation. (*NAC*)

A Panther PzKpfw VA medium tank of the German Army is pictured operating along the Gothic Line in the summer of 1944. In late February 1944, the 'V' was removed from the tanks' designation on the orders of Adolf Hitler, who said they should be called PzKpfw Panthers. The Panther had been developed to counter the Soviet T34 tank and had a main armament of a 75mm L/70 high-velocity gun. (*Author's Collection*)

Below: A group of British Army officers in the vicinity of the German Gothic Line have commandeered horses to go on a reconnaissance of the enemy positions. The Gothic Line was the Germans' last major defence line and it stretched along the summits of the northern Apennine Mountains. Over 1.2 million men were involved in the battle for the German defences, which were manned by the 10th and 14th armies. (*Author's Collection*)

Above: The crew of a 20mm Flakvierling 38 stationed along the Gothic Line fire at low-flying Allied aircraft in the summer of 1944. This four-gun combination was reported to be feared by RAF and USAF pilots due to the concentration of fire that it provided. As the Luftwaffe had virtually lost control of the skies over Italy, these weapons were even more important to the Germans. (*NAC*)

This medium mortar crew of the Waffen SS Reichswehr Division is seen in action on the Gothic Line in the summer of 1944. Formed in November 1943, the division was the only Waffen SS unit to fight in Italy until the formation of the Italia Division in late 1944. During the summer of 1944, a battalion of the division was withdrawn from its defensive positions on the German Gothic Line. One of the reasons that the battalion was chosen was because the Reichswehr had earned a reputation for treating the enemy with great brutality. Many of the volunteers for the unit were transferred from the SS Totenkopf Division, which was responsible for administrating Nazi concentration camps. (*NAC*)

Above: A German Panzerkampfwagen IV Ausf. H medium tank has been positioned under a tree in an Italian village near the Gothic Line. The tank's crew has hastily and rather poorly camouflaged it with house shutters and some tree branches. The Ausf. H had been produced from 1943 and was armed with a 75mm KwK 40 main gun, and its thickest armour was 80mm. (*NAC*)

An Italian partisan who is attached to the Co-Belligerent Motorised Brigade 'Cremona' is armed with a captured MP40 Maschinenpistole 40 sub-machine gun. The pro-Allied 'Cremona' had a strength of 9,000 men, and local partisans like this man would volunteer to perform roles for them. He has been issued with British battledress and a beret with a tricolour ribbon attached, and has the shoulder title 'PARTISAN' sewn on the tunic. (*Author's Collection*)

An 88mm Flak 18 anti-aircraft gun is pushed into position to be used in its secondary role as a highly potent anti-tank gun. The gun had proved itself in the anti-tank role, especially during the North African campaign, but its design gave it a high profile, particularly in the open deserts of Libya and Egypt. However, its long range meant that it could deal with all types of Allied tanks, usually before coming under return fire from them. They were used in large numbers in Italy in the anti-aircraft role in an attempt to compensate for the Allied aerial supremacy. (*Author's Collection*)

German paratroopers rest after fighting off an Allied attack against a village close to Rimini in mid-September. The port on the Adriatic coast had been earmarked by the 8th Army as a possible breakthrough point on the Gothic Line. Many villages on the approaches to the city were fortified by the Germans, who were not going to give ground easily. *(Author's Collection)*

A German anti-tank gun has been positioned on the outskirts of Rimini and is coming under attack from Allied forces in September 1944. The 75mm PAK 40 is camouflaged by foliage and the crew have dug a hole into the surface of the road to provide some shelter. The battle for the Adriatic port lasted from 13 to 21 September and saw a total of 1,470,000 Allied shells fired against it. At the end of the fighting, only 2 per cent of the town's buildings were undamaged after one of the bitterest battles of the campaign. *(Author's Collection)*

A Greek Bren gunner of the 3rd Mountain Division and his infantry escort fire from the shelter of rubble in the centre of Rimini on the Adriatic coast of Italy. They are fighting for control of the town, which fell to the 8th Army on 21 September 1944. Greeks had fought in North Africa and were to go on fighting in Italy until the end of the campaign. *(Author's Collection)*

In the aftermath of the fighting for Rimini in mid to late September 1944, a platoon of German infantry have been taken prisoner in its ruins; they look tired and relieved that their war is over. Other German soldiers were willing to fight to the end on every front and most maintained a good level of morale until the last days of the war. Behind the men is an Mk IV model H medium tank of the German Army, which despite the introduction of the Tiger and Panther tanks was still the main type in service. *(Author's Collection)*

Two heavily armed Fallschirmjägers are pictured during fighting in the southern Apennines in the summer of 1944. They belong to the 4th Parachute Division, which was formed in November 1943, and its first battle was for the Anzio beachhead. The division fought at Futa Pass on the Gothic Line, which was the main route from the German defences to Bologna. Both paratroopers have been issued with plenty of ammunition for the MG42 machine gun and the MP40 sub-machine gun. *(Author's Collection)*

This view from a former German machine-gun hilltop post along the Gothic Line shows Allied trucks on the road below. Although this section of the defensive line is confined to a line of trenches, at other places it was made up of concrete pillboxes. In total, there were 2,000 fortified machine-gun posts, artillery firing positions and bunkers along its length. It was largely built using slave labourers organised by the Todt Organisation, with up to 15,000 forced to work on its defences. *(Author's Collection)*

High in the mountains of central Italy, a German unit looks down into the valley below for advancing Allied troops. They are armed with Italian weaponry, including Carcano M38 carbines and an ex-Italian 47mm Cannone da 47/32 anti-tank or close support gun. This weapon had entered Italian service in 1935 and was fairly outdated by the time Italy entered the war in 1940. Large numbers of these guns had been captured in 1943 by the German Army and were also issued to the newly formed RSI pro-Mussolini forces. Although by 1944 the gun was pretty ineffective against modern Allied armour, they could be used in their secondary role of infantry support. In German service, the gun was known as the 4.7cm Pak 177 and according to photographic evidence was used in large numbers in Italy. (*NAC*)

Indian troops get a lift through a recently captured Italian town aboard an ex-Italian Army 'Lince' – Lynx scout car. There were only 250 of these vehicles produced for the Italian Army and they were based on the British Daimler scout car. Some were taken into service with the German Army after 1943, and this vehicle has German markings. In total, 50,000 Indians fought in Italy, with the three main formations being the 4th, 8th and 10th divisions. (*NAC*)

Soldiers of the Polish II Corps move cautiously through a town to the north of Rimini after the fall of the coastal town in late September. They are pursuing retreating German troops who are withdrawing further north up the Adriatic coast of Italy. The 50,000-strong corps had arrived in Italy with a strong desire for revenge for their fellow countrymen who were under the brutal occupation of the German Army. (*NARA*)

A smiling Nepalese Gurkha proudly shows off his kukri fighting knife, which was synonymous with these Himalayan warriors. Gurkhas fought in the Indian Army, with 110,000 serving on a number of fronts including North Africa, Italy and Burma. There were battalions of Gurkhas in the 4th, 8th and 10th Indian divisions that served in Italy from 1943 to 1945. Although the Gurkhas were known for their high morale and good humour during the campaign, the Italian weather sometimes challenged even their hardiness. (*Author's Collection*)

Platoon commanders of 7th Battalion, Oxford & Bucks Light Infantry Regiment observe enemy positions during the eleven-day battle for the village of Gemmano and the surrounding hills in September 1944. The village had a highly strategic significance because of its dominant position along the Gothic Line. Although the village fell to British forces on the 9th, it took two further attacks to consolidate their hold on their objective. This fierce battle cost the Germans about 900 dead, while British losses were heavier, with every battalion involved suffering an average of 125 dead or wounded. (*Author's Collection*)

Above: The crew of a British Army 3.7-inch anti-aircraft gun fires air burst shells at German and Italian targets along the Gothic Line. A large number of these AA guns were used in this secondary role during the softening up of the enemy defensive positions. It was along the Adriatic coast that the Gothic Line was finally breached in mid-September and the Germans retired to new defences known as the Rimini Line. (*Author's Collection*)

A turret of a Panther tank has been built into a concrete casement as part of the defences of the Gothic Line at Futa Pass in the Apennine Mountains in September 1944. Surplus tank turrets could be ordered straight from the production line due to a shortage of tank hulls to fit them to. Unfortunately for the defenders of the Gothic Line, only four of the thirty Panther turrets arrived in time to be manned in the fighting. (*Author's Collection*)

This German gun position along the Gothic Line is protected by an old Italian gun that had been in service since 1913. The gun is a 65mm Cannone da 65/17, which was used as a mountain gun during the First World War. By 1940, the gun had been withdrawn from Alpini units and the remaining 700 were used in North Africa and the Balkans in 1940 to 1943. In desperation, the 65/17 was put into German service after 1943, and was known in their hands as the GebK 246. Although the gun was supposed to be capable of being used in the anti-tank role, its shells were not very effective against armour. (*NAC*)

These porters carry their loads up a steep hill close to the Futa Pass near the German-held Gothic Line. Although the troops have brought their supplies by mule, some hills were just too steep for the draught animals to climb. Keeping units supplied in Italy often turned into a logistical nightmare where all the motor vehicles available could only get the supplies so far. (*US Army Archives*)

Above: A German soldier moves cautiously up a slope in the vicinity of the Gothic Line in September 1944. The German soldier was usually well trained throughout the war apart from the last few months in 1945, when everything fell apart. It was estimated that the average German soldier was more capable of taking independent actions and was usually encouraged to use their initiative. This man has fixed local foliage to his M35 steel helmet and will crawl across the open field in front of the wood in which he is sheltering. (*Author's Collection*)

The gunner of this German 210mm Mörser 18 heavy howitzer carefully aims towards the Allied positions in central Italy in September 1944. This gun was due to be replaced by the 170mm Kanone 18 in 1942, but the older model remained in German service until the end of the war. Fastened to the barrel of the gun are the charts and tables that allow the aimer to calculate the range he needs to fire accurately. (*NAC*)

Abandoned trenches making up the Gothic Line stretch across the hills of central Italy during the campaign to take the defences in late September 1944. The simple trenches are held in place with wicker screens, with firing positions set up at intervals. Other sections of the Gothic Line had strongpoints and bunkers defended by artillery and machine-gun nests. It was largely the determined attitude of the German defenders aided by Fascist Italians that made the defences so difficult to capture. (*US Army Archives*)

The arrival in July 1944 of the Brazilian Expeditionary Corps – 'Smoking Snakes' – saw a 25,334-strong contingent from South America fighting alongside the 8th and US 5th armies in Italy. They joined the US 5th Army and after some extra training and acclimatisation, they went into action on 6 September and performed well. In this photograph, the officer in the centre is Brigadier General Euclydes Zenobia da Costa, the assistant division commander of the BEC. He points out potential targets when visiting the front line while his officers take notes. (*Author's Collection*)

A Bren gunner of the Co-Belligerent 68th Regiment of the 'Legnano' Gruppo di Combattimento (Legnano Combat Group) poses proudly for the camera. The Legnano was raised on 23 July 1944 and was made up of the 68th Infantry Regiment, a Special Infantry regiment, a service group and the 11th Artillery Regiment. Like most of the Co-Belligerent soldiers, he has been issued with British battledress with steel helmet and has the black collar patches edged in blue. (*Author's Collection*)

Lieutenant Gino Coletti of the Italian Co-Belligerent forces receives a battle honour for his unit, the 9th Arditi Battalion. He is being presented with the award by Major Edoardo Di Stefano of the 68th Infantry Regiment of the 'Legnano' Gruppo di Combattimento. Some Co-Belligerent formations were kept away from the front line by the Allies while others were sent into the front line. (*Author's Collection*)

Chapter Eleven

1943-45
Italy's Civil War

While the Italian Campaign was ongoing, there was another vicious campaign underway in Italy that affected the outcome of the conventional fighting. Italian armed resistance to the German occupation and Mussolini's Salò Republic began after the dictator's fall in July 1943. A new pro-Allied government was set up by Marshal Badoglio but the left-wing National Liberation Committee (Comitato di Liberazione Nazionale, CLN) did not join it. The CLN was a left-wing coalition involving all the anti-Fascist parties of Italy who did not support the continued rule of King Victor Emmanuel. During most of Mussolini's twenty years of rule, there had been political opposition to his regime. From the mid-1920s, any political opposition had been largely countered by Mussolini's police and secret police. In March 1944, the Italian King Victor Emmanuel was formally recognised by the Soviet Union and everything changed. It was now regarded as acceptable for communists and other left-wingers to join the government and fight the mutual enemy. From September 1943, a number of armed bands had been organised in occupied Italy with volunteers from various anti-Fascist political parties. These parties included some that had existed since before the rise of Mussolini or had come into underground politics since the 1930s: Communists, Socialists, Liberals, Christian Democrats, Labour Democrats and the members of the Action Party. Having spent their time trying to avoid the attentions of Mussolini's secret police, these left-wingers now saw the chance to fight the Fascist regime and the German occupiers.

The Communists formed the largest number of partisan bands – 'Garibaldini' brigades – while Socialists raised 'Matteotti' brigades, named after the politician murdered by Fascists in the 1920s. Other bands were formed from members of the Action Party, which were known as the 'Liberty and Justice' brigades. At first, the total number of partisans was low, with only 9,000 in December 1943, but by the following March there were 25,000. The number of active fighters in the field by June 1944 had reached 80,000, and by the end of the war, there were 250,000 Italian partisans. This total included the usual hangers-on who picked up a rifle as the war drew to a close to identify themselves with the victors. Hardcore partisans had been fighting in the hills and mountains of Italy since 1943, and these groups managed to control large tracts of countryside by 1944. In northern Italy, a number of Partisan Republics sprang up from 1943 and acted as temporary mini-republics. There were about eleven of these republics, including the Alba, Torriglia, Ossola, Carnia and Montefiorno republics. Despite valiant resistance, these Partisan Republics were soon overrun by German and Italian Fascist forces, with the partisans retreating back into the mountains. The Republic of Ossola, on the Swiss border, had a population of 82,000 people, but like all the others, it fell to an Axis offensive. Also fighting on the Allied side since 1943 was the rapidly expanding pro-Allied Co-Belligerent Army, armed and trained by the British and US armies. This army fluctuated in size from 190,000 to 244,000 men by 1945, and was gradually incorporated into the front line to replace Allied units.

Facing the partisan threat by 1944–45 were a mixture of German troops withdrawn from the front line and large numbers of armed Italian Fascists. Many Italians were still willing to fight for Mussolini and his puppet government established in northern Italy in 1943. Fascist troops comprised the 52,000-strong National Republican Army (ENR), with four regular divisions. The former pre-1943 MVSN Fascist military organisation was recreated as the Guardia Nazionale Repubblicana (GNR), with 80,000 volunteers. In addition, there was the large number of battalion-sized Black Brigades, with most active Fascist members, totalling 110,000 disciplined and well-armed men and women. There were so many armed Fascist groups in central and northern Italy during the Civil War that the estimated figure of 520,000 volunteers may well be close to the truth. Units were formed in cities, towns and villages by the local Fascist politicians, who dealt with any suspected left-wingers who had not already fled to join the partisans. Many atrocities were committed during the Civil War, with at least 80,500 civilians being killed between 1943 and 1945. German occupation troops ran their own anti-partisan campaign, often with the support of Italian Fascists. The partisans had the dual role of disrupting the German war machine throughout Italy and fighting their Fascist enemies. With no quarter given, the guerrilla fighting in northern Italy reached new levels of brutality in the last months of the Italian Campaign. At the end of the war, many defeated Fascists were shot, including many of the regime's corrupt leaders who were long hated by the opposition. High-profile Fascists who had supported Mussolini were also killed, especially those who continued to support him after his fall from power in 1943. The executed included several film stars and other celebrities whose public roles were considered by the left wing to be part of the support for Fascist society and the Salò Republic. In an effort to escape a similar fate, some right-wing Italians and Fascists tried to join the partisans in the last week of the war, mostly unsuccessfully. The Civil War was a particularly brutal conflict with heavy losses on both sides, with the partisans suffering 35,828 killed and over 21,000 wounded. On the Fascist side, the losses were similar, with 13,170 dead and 21,600 wounded, as well as an unknown number dealt with in its aftermath.

Three anti-German fighters have taken to the woods in the summer of 1943, beginning what was to develop into a major partisan campaign. They appear to be ex-Italian Army soldiers who still wear their former uniforms, although they are armed with German rifles and grenades. When the pre-1943 Italian Army broke up, some of its soldiers chose to 'take to the hills' and fight the German occupiers and their Italian Fascist allies. (*Author's Collection*)

These Alpini operating in the mountains of northern Italy in the autumn of 1944 belong to the Valanga Battalion of the 'X' MAS Autonomous unit, which was the size of a regular division. This elite division was raised outside the establishment of the original four divisions raised in Germany from October 1943. It took part in anti-partisan operations in northern Italy, especially in the autumn and winter of 1944/45. By April 1944, the division had grown to 25,000 men and was probably the most effective Fascist formation still fighting for Mussolini until the end of the war in Italy. (*Author's Collection*)

A quad 20mm Flakvierling 38 anti-aircraft gun of the German Army fires into the mountains where they suspect Italian partisans are based. In many cases, the Germans left fighting partisans over the winter of 1944/45 to the armed forces of the Salò Republic. Most German formations were fully occupied in fighting the Allied armies and saw the Italian resistance as a troublesome distraction. (*Author's Collection*)

German anti-guerrilla troops clamber up a steep hill in the summer of 1944 in search of Italian partisans in their mountain bases. Thousands of Italian men had taken to the hills after September 1943 to avoid forced conscription as workers to be sent to Nazi Germany. Although many partisans were not initially politicised, once in the ranks of the anti-Fascist fighters they soon aligned with left-wing political parties. The dominant political allegiance amongst the partisans was to the Italian Communist Party. (*NAC*)

A German Waffen SS volunteer armed with an MP40 sub-machine gun is pictured during an anti-partisan operation in northern Italy in 1944. While the Germans were desperately defending central and northern Italy from the Allied armies in 1944 and 1945, they were faced by resistance that grew stronger as the campaign progressed. Fighting against the partisans continued until the end of the fighting in Europe in early May 1945. *(Author's Collection)*

A 25-year-old partisan leader proudly posing for the camera having just captured a Fascist leader. He belongs to a pro-Communist Garibaldini partisan group, shown by the red star on his British Army beret and the red scarf around his neck. His arms are from a number of sources, with a donated British Sten sub-machine gun, an Italian Beretta 34 pistol and a German stick grenade. *(Author's Collection)*

Two Guardia Nazionale Repubblicana militiamen pose for the camera as they are defending a railway line during the fighting with the partisans in the summer of 1944. The GNR, like its predecessor the MVSN, had units responsible for defending the infrastructure of the Fascist Salò Republic. Most volunteers of the GNR were, not surprisingly, made up of ex-MVSN militiamen. Family loyalty meant that the GNR and the Black Brigades were often filled with fathers and sons who were still loyal to Benito Mussolini. (*Author's Collection*)

A group of partisans poses for a studio photograph wearing uniforms taken from Italian stores, and most appear to be dressed in tropical shirts and shorts. In the later stages of the campaign, a number of partisan units were as well dressed as this group of anti-Fascist fighters. Many of them are armed with British Sten sub-machine guns while the rest have Italian Army Carcano carbines. (*Author's Collection*)

Looking like a group of bandits from Renaissance Italy, these partisans are operating in the hills around Cisterna in Cassino Province in 1944. They are working to support the newly established Anzio bridgehead by attacking German supply lines running up to the front. The man on the left is armed with a newly issued Maschinenkarabiner 42H while his comrades have a British Sten gun and a German MP40 sub-machine gun. (*Author's Collection*)

A group of Italian partisans are pictured during an operation against the German or Italian Fascists in support of the Allies in the summer of 1944. Most of the partisans are wearing cast-off Italian tropical uniforms to which they had have added their own red star insignia. Most partisan groups were affiliated to left-wing or liberal Italian political parties that had been banned by Mussolini's Fascist regime. (*Author's Collection*)

A partisan fighter has been dealt with by local Fascist militiamen who tied him to a tree and shot him after beating him. As a brutal warning to the population, a placard has been nailed to the tree, with the warning: 'This will be the end of all partisans and anti-German spies!!!' This was the reality for any captured partisan, and similar treatment could be expected by any Fascist falling into enemy hands. (*Author's Collection*)

Young Fascist volunteers of the 'Ettore Muti' Autonomous Mobile Legion on parade on the streets of Milan on 29 October. The legion was named after the famous fighter pilot and bodyguard of Mussolini, Ettore Muti, who was seen as the ultimate example of Fascist machismo. It had begun life as a squad and then expanded rapidly to reach a strength of 1,600 youths and men. On the collarless tunic is a black cloth patch with a red fasces and silver metal skull and crossbones. (*Author's Collection*)

Smartly uniformed GNR volunteers are seen on parade after the formation of their militia unit armed with Beretta M1938A sub-machine guns. Many of the GNR volunteers came from the ranks of elite units like the Carabinieri (military police) and the now inactive Polizia dell'Africa Italiana (PAI). These veterans brought their attitude to order, discipline and smartness to the GNR, which was followed by the younger volunteers, many of whom had not seen military service. (*Author's Collection*)

Fascist GNR volunteers patrol the streets of Milan in the autumn of 1944. They are riding in the Italian-made Sahariana armoured cars, which were designed for service in desert conditions. The Fiat-Spa Camionetta S43s that survived the war in North Africa saw service with the Italian Fascist forces post-1943. They were armed with a 20mm anti-aircraft gun used in the ground role, and several light machine guns. Fascist forces had limited numbers of tanks, armoured vehicles and artillery, but the majority of fighting was done by infantry groups on both sides of the Civil War. *(Author's Collection)*

A unit of Italian partisans gather in a town square to show off their equipment and weaponry. This particular unit is working in close support of the advancing Allied forces and the fighters have been issued with British Army khaki wool uniforms. Their weaponry, which is made up of German MG42s and Italian Breda 30 machine guns, has either been captured by the partisans or given to them as 'war booty' by the 8th Army. *(Author's Collection)*

A group of Fascist Black Brigade volunteers on patrol in a civilian car in 1944 around Val D'Ossola in Novara province. The other ranks wear black shirts or pullovers with light khaki tropical trousers and steel helmets, which are Greek models captured in 1941. The officer in the centre wears an Italian Army bustina side cap while the man with binoculars has a German-style field cap. (*Author's Collection*)

GNR volunteers are pictured in this dramatically staged action shelling suspected partisans in 1944 with an 81mm mortar. The pro-Fascist militias that proliferated in northern Italy from 1943 were given sufficient small arms and light artillery to fight the partisans. Heavier weaponry was in shorter supply and most leftover Italian tanks and heavy artillery was out of date even when available. (*Author's Collection*)

An officer and machine-gunner of the 'Picot' Black Brigade take part in training during their anti-partisan campaign in 1944. The officer is armed with a TZ 45 sub-machine gun, which was produced in Italy in small numbers. Their machine gun is a Fiat 1914/35, which was a poor weapon, a badly modified version of the 1914 heavy machine gun. Nevertheless, this machine gun was the main type in service with the Italian Army from 1935 until 1945. (*Author's Collection*)

A Black Brigade gathers in a town square in northern Italy in the autumn of 1944; the members are wearing the distinctive black caps and shirt with surplus army trousers. These militia were recruited largely from the older Fascists who had served in the pre-1943 MVSN. Other volunteers were made up of pro-Mussolini discharged soldiers and youths and even children who remained loyal to the Italian dictator. (*Author's Collection*)

Allesandro Pavolini, in the black shirt and cap, was a high-ranking Fascist official who was part of Mussolini's inner circle and remained loyal to him until the end. He took command of the Brigate Nere – Black Brigades – when they were first formed in June 1944. Here he is inspecting some of the 30,000 volunteers of the Black Brigades, which were tasked with keeping control of the Italian population and fighting partisans. (*Author's Collection*)

This Fascist propaganda photograph shows a firefight between Black Brigade volunteers and partisans in the autumn of 1944. The Black Brigade silver metal skull and crossbones badge can clearly be seen on the front of the black field cap. This hat, known as the *beretto di campagna*, was based on the field cap worn by much of the German Army in 1944. The soldier is armed with the Beretta M38A sub-machine gun, which was one of the few Italian weapons that was as good if not better than other weapons of its kind. (*Author's Collection*)

Two commanders of the 'Garibaldini' Communist partisans pose for the camera in the summer of 1944. They wear a mix of captured and adapted uniforms, with the man on the left having the two-star rank of lieutenant on his chest. He also wears an ex-Fascist field cap. On the front of his cap, he has fixed a tricolour star, while his fellow officer has the three stars, showing he is a captain. (*Author's Collection*)

Chapter Twelve

September 1944–January 1945
The Last Winter

As the 8th and US 5th armies advanced northwards from the Gothic Line in late September 1944, the gathering Italian winter weather was already affecting the campaign. The severe conditions, including torrential rain, favoured the German defence as they hunkered down in their various fortified positions. Hitler had issued Kesselring with the strict order that the German Army should not withdraw north of the Po River. Although the fall of Rimini came as a blow to the Germans, the 10th Army withdrew in order to take up new positions behind the Marecchia River. Kesselring himself was despondent and he confided to his staff officers that he thought the situation in Italy was 'sliding'. The 8th Army was confident after their victory at Rimini and fully expected to push into the open country of the Romagna. An attack across the Marecchia River on 22 September by New Zealand troops was successful against the 162nd Turkoman Division. They then came up against more resolute troops of the 1st Parachute Division and their attack ground to a halt. In thirty-six hours, the paratroopers fought off twenty-seven battalion strength attacks by the New Zealanders. For several days, teeming rain fell along the contested river and it did not stop until 3 October. While the 8th Army was totally bogged down, the US 5th Army, advancing in the centre of the front, was still looking to move against its main objective, Bologna. The US 5th Army had been moving towards the towns of Imola and Faenza but were making little real progress. On 28 September, General Clark decided to switch all of the 5th Army's emphasis to taking Bologna. Clark's units were now suffering from a lack of frontline personnel, with losses of 550 men per day being irreplaceable. These shortages caused consternation and frustration for Clark as, by 2 October, his men were only 20 miles from the city. A week later, some of his vanguard troops were only 10 miles from Bologna city centre but could not get any further. Both armies had suffered heavy casualties, with at least 20,000 men killed since the fall of Cassino in May. Heavy rain again affected the fighting in Italy and the rain continued to fall during the rest of October. It turned the roads into streams and streams into rivers, with bridges swept away and motor vehicles constantly stuck in deep mud. The difficulty of moving supplies around now led to shortages of ammunition and other war material at the front. As shortages of ammunition at the front line were becoming critical, the US 5th Army was not capable of operating on a war footing. By the 28th of the month, things had deteriorated to a point where the offensive had to be closed down and the 5th Army began to hunker down for winter.

The 8th Army was suffering from the same problems as the US 5th Army but their advance continued past the end of October. Their main objective was to catch up with the US 5th Army and stabilise the front for the expected final offensive once the weather improved. Some limited breakthroughs were achieved by the 8th Army, with the Savio River being crossed on 7 November and the Lamone River reached on the 16th. Fighting continued on a lower level on the 8th Army front throughout December in ever worsening conditions. On 4 December, the city of Ravenna was taken, and on the 16th, the German stronghold of Faenza fell. As usual, the Germans had prepared defences further north and their forces were on the far bank of the Senio River. Neither side had the strength or determination to continue large-scale actions; by 29 December, all Allied attacks halted for the winter. It was not that there was an official ceasefire in place, but fighting in the winter conditions was simply becoming too difficult for both adversaries.

A wire photo features a Maori Bren gunner of the New Zealand 2nd Division of the 8th Army, which is about to cross the Fiumicino River on 1 October 1944. Once across the river, the 8th Army clashed with German formations in the Savignano area. This soldier appears to have acquired a German paratrooper's helmet that formerly belonged to the 1st Fallschirmjäger Division, which was active in Italy until May 1945. (*Author's Collection*)

This lance corporal belongs to the Esercito Nazionale Repubblicano (ENR), which was the army of the pro-Mussolini government in northern Italy. He belongs to the 'Army Group Liguria', which was the main pro-German Italian military formation that fought on the defence line. This formation, under the command of General Rodolfo Graziani, comprised the Italian 3rd 'San Marco' Marine Division and the 4th 'Monterosa' Mountain Division. The army was bolstered by the addition of the German 34th Infantry Division and the 42nd Jäger Division. The soldier has an ex-Italian Royal Army M1940 uniform on with the RSI gladio sword and laurel wreath metal badge on the lapel. His main armament is a Beretta M1938A sub-machine gun as well as a Beretta M1934 automatic pistol. In his right hand is a red-painted Modello 35 grenade, which came in three variants, all given the name 'red devils' for obvious reasons. (*Author's Collection*)

A German soldier manning the Gothic Line in October 1944 takes the opportunity to eat an apple during a break in fighting. By his uniform, he appears to be a Panzergrenadier of one of the two divisions fighting along the defence line in October 1944. Three of the best German units in Italy, the 29th and 90th Panzergrenadier divisions and the 1st Parachute Division were part of the Gothic Line defence force. (*NAC*)

Indian Army Gurkhas cross the Ronco River on 28 October 1944, using ropes to steady themselves as they wade across. Once the far bank of the river had been secured, a Bailey bridge was built to span it and allow vehicles across. The capture of Rimini was followed by an advance to the Ronco, where the Germans were waiting 2 miles to the east of the town of Forli. These Indian Army troops have found a stretch of the Ronco further south that was lightly defended, allowing them to cross. (*Author's Collection*)

This photograph, taken in October 1944, illustrates the difficulty of supplying the front lines in the rainy season. The sign nailed up at the side of Route 6531, which has been turned into a quagmire, is to the point. It reminds the US supply drivers to try to avoid the old ruts or they will probably end up stuck, waiting to be towed out by tracked vehicles. (*Author's Collection*)

The importance of mules to the Allied armies in Italy cannot be overstressed, as there were so many situations where they were the only means of supply. During the advance up the Italian peninsula, the Germans constantly had the main roads in their gunsights and often, other routes over open country had to be taken. This mule column of the US 5th Army moves gingerly up a rocky slope with ammunition and other vital supplies on the animals' backs. In this case, the mules are having to climb several hundred feet up to avoid coming under fire from German artillery. (*Author's Collection*)

During fighting in November 1944, Polish Engineers prepare an explosive charge in the shelter of a gully. In the background, one of their comrades is having his hand bandaged after a recent clash by his unit with the Germans. The Polish contingent in Italy was largely made up of former prisoners of the Soviet Union captured during the invasion of 1939. It took a while for the Polish to be properly equipped and armed by the Allies but eventually, a II Corps was formed. Rising to 110,000 men, the Polish II Corps fought at Monte Cassino, as well as other battles. During the Italian Campaign, the II Corps suffered 2,301 men killed in action and 8,543 wounded, with another 535 missing. (*Author's Collection*)

Below: A light machine-gunner of the Italian Republican Army aims his obsolete Breda 30 light machine gun towards Allied lines in November 1944. He and his comrades are holding positions in the Emilian Apennines, a mountainous region that is in the southern region of northern Italy. Once the defensive lines held by these Italian Fascists and German troops had fallen, then the last Italian cities in Axis hands would be open to attack. (*Author's Collection*)

These Italian volunteers of the 29th Waffen Grenadier SS Division are seen manning the Gothic Line in December 1944. They are armed with former Italian Army M38 carbines, and wear their M33 steel helmets and camouflage capes. Some volunteers of the division took part in a successful offensive against the Allied-held towns of Massa and Lucca in late December, codenamed Operation Winter Storm. Axis losses during the offensive, which was aimed at a western section of the Gothic Line, totalled 1,000. (*Author's Collection*)

A paratrooper of the 1st Parachute Division pushes a wheelbarrow down a muddy path with an ammunition box loaded in it. The terrible conditions faced by both sides during the fighting for the Gothic Line can be seen. Any idea that fighting on the Italian Font was an easy option for Axis or Allied troops would be dispelled by photographs like this. (*NAC*)

British soldiers of the 8th Army drag a searchlight from the back of a truck ready to be mounted on a wheeled carriage in heavy mud. According to the original caption of this photograph, this searchlight is not going to be used in an anti-aircraft role. Instead it is intended to light up mountain roads for the army's transport trucks to try to avoid them crashing or even falling off the mountain. (*Author's Collection*)

During the stalemate in Italy, largely caused by the winter conditions, the US Army is using this abandoned farmhouse as a repair facility for armoured vehicles. Some damaged tanks could be repaired at improvised garages like this, which is a few hundred yards behind the front line. This group of armoured vehicles includes three Sherman M4s, two M18 self-propelled guns and an M3 tank recovery vehicle. (*US Army Archives*)

This mortar crew of the US 92nd Afro-American Infantry Division are fighting for control of the town of Massa in late December 1944. The fighting is part of the Axis Operation Winter Storm, which was known by the Allies as the Battle of Garfagnana. During the brutal three-day battle from 26 to 28 December, the Allies lost 1,000 men. The 92nd Division, known as 'Buffalo Soldiers', was formed in October 1917 and took part in the First World War. During the Italian Campaign, the division fought from the Gothic Line in 1944 until the fall of the Po Valley in the spring of 1945. (*US Army Archives*)

This propaganda poster issued by the Salò Republic appeals to Italian men to fight alongside their German allies in 1944. The Italian Bersaglieri and German Waffen SS volunteer point at the onlooker and say: *'E TU.. COSA FAI?'* ('And you … what are you doing?'). Many Fascist supporters did not need much persuasion to fight for Mussolini's puppet state in northern Italy. By 1944, the country was deeply divided into pro-Fascist and anti-Fascist camps. (*Author's Collection*)

Soldiers of the Italian Republican Army belonging to the 4th Division 'Alpini' Monterosa man a 47mm anti-tank gun on 18 December 1944. The regular units of the RSI Armed Forces had been largely recruited from prisoner of war camps in Germany and occupied Italy. As the Italian Campaign drew to a close, units like this were still willing to fight alongside their German counterparts. Their Cannone da 47/32 M35 was a licence-built version of the Austrian Böhler anti-tank gun. It was the main anti-tank gun of the Italian Army in 1940 and had a secondary role of close support gun. (*Author's Collection*)

For most soldiers on the Italian Front in the winter of 1944/45, bivouacs like this were home while waiting for better weather to arrive. Soldiers became expert scavengers, and most did all they could to make even a temporary camp as comfortable as possible. Of course, both sides suffered during the extreme cold weather, but in most cases, the supply system for the Allies was now better than for the Germans. (*Author's Collection*)

In the midst of the winter of 1944/45, an American soldier covered in snow fills petrol cans from a tanker. He is preparing the cans to be picked up by US military drivers passing as they move up the Raticosa Pass along Highway 65 to the south of the city of Bologna. This petrol supply station is situated at the end of the pipeline that ran from the port of Livorno on the western coast of Tuscany. (*US Army Archives*)

American soldiers use their spare time during a lull in the fighting in the deep winter of 1944/45 to cut logs for their campfires. Both armies struggled to keep the level of fighting up during the winter months and most skirmishes were at small unit level. The hot summers and cold winters of Italy presented a number of practical difficulties for the Axis and Allied armies. *(US National Archives)*

A British Grenadier Guard fighting with the US 5th Army in the mountains of northern Italy in the winter of 1944/45. He is aiming with his Lee Enfield No. 4 rifle at a German sniper, who presumably is wearing a white snowsuit. This two-piece snowsuit was issued to many British and US soldiers in time for the winter campaigning of 1944/45. *(Author's Collection)*

German paratroopers reinforce their defensive position with extra barbed wire in the snow of the Italian winter. During the winter of 1944/45, Kesselring tried to keep his men active by undertaking this kind of work. His men were busy building trenches and other defence works along every river on the Allies' route into northern Italy. By the end of the winter, the 1st Parachute Corps still had a strength of 30,000 men and was to prove a redoubtable foe for the 8th and US 5th armies. (*Author's Collection*)

These German paratroopers advance through a snow-covered Italian town in the winter of 1944/45. A few months before, the 4th Parachute Division had been part of the German force that managed to halt an Allied advance by the 2nd Corps south of the city of Bologna. These so-called 'Green Devils' gained a fearsome reputation as ground troops after large-scale airborne operations were cancelled following the devastating losses suffered in the invasion of Crete in May 1941. (*Author's Collection*)

British artillerymen clear their 25-pounder field gun of snow in the long winter of 1944/45. First used in action in Norway in 1940, the 25-pounder became the main medium howitzer of the British Army and 12,000 were produced before 1945. During the North Africa Campaign of 1940–43, it was used as an anti-tank gun, but in most theatres it was only used as a field gun. It was known for its ruggedness and reliability, and the German Army used them in large numbers after having captured them in France in 1940. *(Author's Collection)*

A mule column of the US 10th Mountain Division moves across snowy country during the winter of 1944/45. Mules were vital for the Allied supply line on several fronts during the Second World War. They were heavily engaged in Burma and the Far East from 1943 to 1945, as well as in Italy during the same period. At the same time, new uniforms were being introduced into Allied service and these American soldiers have been issued with new winter uniforms, including fur hats. (*US Army Archives*)

The driver of an M29 Weasel checks that his vehicle is not bogged down as it moves along a muddy Italian road. This cross-country vehicle was designed for use in snow but it was equally useful in the muddy conditions found in Italy. Weasels usually had a crew of two and they could carry a load of approximately 1,000 pounds. (*US Army Archives*)

The leader of a US Army patrol, Sergeant Caraway, is in the mountains north of Pracchia and stops at the side of a road for a cigarette on 7 December. Pracchia, in Tuscany, was a small hamlet during the Italian Campaign but German troops often fortified villages like this during the Allied advance in 1944. The soldier has taped two Thompson sub-machine gun 30-round magazines together to switch them when his first runs out of bullets. (*US Army Archives*)

This Marder III Ausf. M tank destroyer is parked at the entrance of a tunnel on 21 December 1944. The tank destroyer, which was produced in large numbers, was based on the chassis of the ex-Czech PzKpfw 38 (T) medium tank. Its commander checks for Allied movements with his binoculars during a lull in the fighting for northern Italy. (*NAC*)

Prince Junio Valerio Borghese, the charismatic commander of the 'X MAS' autonomous unit, inspects some of his men on 8 January 1945. The prince had been in command of a special pre-Armistice navy attack unit, the '10th Anti-Submarine Motorboat Flotilla'. When Italy surrendered, he immediately offered his services to Germany and was highly successful in raising the 'X MAS', which eventually grew to 25,000 and included women's units. In front of the men is a row of Model 37 heavy machine guns – a poorly designed Italian weapon introduced in the late 1930s. (*Author's Collection*)

Officers of the 'Bergamo' Alpini Battalion of the Italian Republican Army's 'Littorio' Division gather for a parade in northern Italy on 31 January. The Alpini were widely regarded as the elite of the pre-1943 Italian Army and units were raised to serve in the post-1943 Republican Army. Ranks of the Alpini were shown on the left side of the hat with braiding, and also with the type of feather attached to them. (*Author's Collection*)

Benito Mussolini stands on top of the turret of an Italian M14/41 medium tank to make a speech to the men of the 'Leonessa' Tank Group on 17 December 1944 in Milan. The 'Leonessa' was the main armoured unit of the Guardia Nazionale Repubblicana and was equipped with a variety of Italian armoured vehicles. This was one of the last public appearances of the Italian dictator, who had been reduced to being a powerless figurehead of the Fascist Salò Republic. (*Author's Collection*)

Below: In February 1945, a unit of partisans attend a ceremony at which their commander is being awarded an Italian bravery medal. They belong to the 28th 'Mario Gordini' Garibaldini Brigade, which was commanded by the Communist politician Arrigo Boldrini. Like other well-organised partisan brigades, the fighters of the 28th have been issued with some British military uniforms, which they are wearing with civilian items. The tricolour rosettes on their army issue berets were a feature of partisan uniforms, and the men are armed with Lee Enfield No. 4 rifles and a Sten Mk 2 sub-machine gun. (*Author's Collection*)

Chapter Thirteen

April 1945
The Allied Spring Offensive

After the lull in fighting during the long Italian winter of 1944/45, both sides girded their loins for the coming spring fighting. In early March 1945, the German Army in northern Italy was still under the command of General Kesselring. He still had twenty-three divisions available for the defence of what was left of 'unoccupied' Italy despite losing the 16th SS Panzer Division and three Infantry divisions to the Western and Eastern Front. Kesselring was determined to resist any further reductions in his strength as he prepared to meet the Allied offensive. He had the 26th Panzer Division, 20th and 90th Panzergrenadier divisions, two Parachute, two Jäger, three Mountain and thirteen Infantry divisions. All of the Jäger, Mountain and Infantry divisions had been reduced in size by 1,700 men. He also had two divisions of the Italian Republican 'Army of Liguria' under the command of Marshal Graziani. The Allied Supreme Commander General Clark had seventeen divisions at his disposal in Italy in March 1945. Nine divisions were in the US 5th Army, with two Armoured – the 1st US and 6th South African divisions – and 5 were Infantry. In addition, there was one division of Brazilian troops of the Brazilian Expeditionary Corps (BEC) and the US 10th Mountain Division trained for fighting in the mountains of northern Italy. Clark also had the eight divisions of the 8th Army, including three British (6th Armoured and 50th and 78th Infantry divisions), and two Indian divisions (the 8th and 10th). The other three divisions were two Polish (the 3rd and 8th) and the 2nd New Zealand Division. There were also a number of Independent brigades, which included the 2nd Parachute Brigade and the 2nd Commando Brigade. Other brigades were the Jewish Brigade and two brigades of Co-Belligerent Italians, as well as a number of other less reliable Italian units stationed in quiet sectors of the front.

The German positions in northern Italy were concentrated on defending the many rivers and canals that ran across the Italian peninsula between the Senio River and Bologna. These rivers, the Santerno, Sillaro, Idice and Fossa Cembalina, could all be fortified by the Germans. Any Allied offensive would have to cross these defended rivers before they could reach the Po River and valley and the cities of northern Italy. The Allied Spring Offensive in northern Italy began on 9 April 1945 with a bombing raid by 234 USAF medium bombers, which dropped 24,000 20lb incendiary bombs. This was followed by attacks by 740 fighter-bombers of the US Tactical Air Force against German machine-gun and mortar positions. In a final wave of attacks, 825 heavy bombers dropped 1,692 bombs over the German defence positions at Lugo. As the Germans tried to pull themselves together after the aerial bombardment, the Allied artillery started. A forty-two-minute bombardment by 1,500 guns then began and was followed by a further four similar bombardments. While an isolated attack against La Spezia that began on 5 April continued, a series of attacks in the centre and east of the German defence lines commenced. On 9 April, 8th Army attacked in earnest towards Ferrara via the Argenta Gap and towards Bologna via Imola. By the 12th, it had got bridges across the Santerno River and was also pushing along the north bank of the Reno River. The 5th Army began its moves in the centre on 14 April when they crossed the Senio River heading for Modena, Bologna, Florence and Pistoia.

Meanwhile, the 8th Army in the east also crossed the river, heading for Bologna, Argenta and Ferrara. The Allied troops crossed the Senio over a series of three Bailey bridges, having benefited from four months of training during the late winter and early spring. The 8th Indian Division crossed the Santerno River, while the amphibious carriers of the 9th Armoured Brigade and the 56th Infantry Division crossed the shallows of Lake Comacchio. These troops crossed the lake and outflanked the German positions at Argenta and the Reno River. On 17 April, the British V Corps captured Argenta, and two days later, the 5th Army broke out of the Apennines onto the Po Plateau. The German position was now desperate, having lost most of their heavy artillery and tanks. Thousands of Germans had crossed the Po River, with many, including generals, having to swim across. They were being pursued by US and British tanks, which for the first time during the Italian Campaign had open ground to cross. Bologna fell to the 8th Army on the 21st, having already been largely liberated by Italian partisans. Soldiers of the US 5th Army entered Bologna a few hours later, following the two-pronged Allied attacks against the city. On the 22nd, the 5th Army took Modena, and the following day, advanced units from both armies reached the Po. On the 24th, Ferrara fell and Allied units began to stream across the Po in force towards the Italian borders with Austria, Switzerland and Yugoslavia. While the Allies advanced against scant German opposition, two more big cities in the north, Milan and Turin, had been liberated by Italian partisans. The surrender of German forces in Italy had been inevitable since early April and a series of secret negotiations had taken place. These were led by SS General Karl Wolff, with the assistance of Cardinal Schuster of Milan. An unconditional surrender was duly signed on 29 April and over 1 million German and Italian Fascist troops gave up the fight. In total, twenty-two German divisions and six Italian Fascist divisions surrendered in northern Italy and across the border in Austria.

German artillery prepare their gun under the cover of a camouflage net to protect them from Allied air attack. As the fighting in Italy was coming to an end, the desperate Germans employed any available weaponry. This gun is an ex-Czech 100mm Model 30, which was usually employed by the Germans as a coastal gun. In the German Army, it was given the designation *leichte Feldhaubitze 30* (light field howitzer 30), and some found their way to Italy. (*Author's Collection*)

As the campaign in Italy drew to a close in early 1945, limited German reinforcements were sent to bolster the defences there. This photograph illustrates well the growing shortages in weapons and equipment in the German Army in late 1944 and early 1945. The soldiers are driving an ex-Austrian Army Saurer RK7 tracked and wheeled light artillery tractor. This vehicle may well have been put into storage after the 1938 Anschluss but limited production did continue for the Wehrmacht. (*Author's Collection*)

General Heinrich von Vietinghoff (1887–1952) was in command of the 5th Panzer Division during the Polish campaign in September 1939. He was promoted to the rank of general in June 1940 before fighting on the Eastern Front in command of the 2nd Panzer Army from December 1941 to August 1943. He was then made commander of the 10th Army in Italy and was responsible for the defence of central Italy. He was put in temporary command of Army Group C when Field Marshal Kesselring was injured. In January 1945, von Vietinghoff was sent to command troops in East Prussia before returning to Italy to take command of all units there when Kesselring left the country in March to take a command in France. From March until early May 1945, von Vietinghoff was the Supreme Commander Italy. (*Author's Collection*)

The commander-in-chief of the Army of the Salò Republic, Marshal Graziani, inspects troops of 'Army Group Liguria'. This formation was made up of Italian troops still loyal to Benito Mussolini, along with the German 34th Infantry Division and the 134th Infantry Brigade. Graziani was photographed on 29 March and just over a month later, on 1 May, he ordered all the troops under his command to lay down their arms. (*Author's Collection*)

General Field Marshal Albert Kesselring was affectionately known as 'Uncle Albert' by his troops. This popularity with his men was largely based on his constant visits to frontline units throughout his career in the Second World War. He is pictured on a visit to a German Airborne Division that was still fighting in the spring of 1945. Kesselring had been injured in a motor accident in late October 1944 and had returned to his duties in January 1945. In the closing stages of the war in Europe, in March 1945, Kesselring was given command of German forces in Eastern Europe as well as in Italy. (*Author's Collection*)

Volunteers of the 29th Waffen-Grenadier Division der SS 'Italienische Nr. 1' are seen on parade in the closing stages of the Italian Campaign armed with Beretta M38 sub-machine guns. Service in what was the Italian branch of the Waffen SS was surprisingly popular, with 15,000 initially coming forward to join. Out of this large number of Italian volunteers a 2,950-strong division was formed, with the unit's NCOs and officers being seconded from the German SS. The unit trained in Germany in the autumn of 1943 and returned to Italy in January 1944. By September 1944, the unit had grown to 6,000 men and it fought until the end of the war in May 1945, mainly in the anti-partisan role. *(Author's Collection)*

This Bren gunner is part of a special battalion size unit of British troops trained in mountain warfare for the fighting in the Italian mountains. He carries equipment that weighs up to 100lb as well as the light machine gun, which weighs 23lb. The weight he is bearing is about half that carried by one of the mules used by the Allies in Italy from 1943 to 1945. (*Author's Collection*)

The crew of an MG42 machine gun peer out from the inside of a house in a town in northern Italy in early 1945. MG42s were the best machine guns in the Second World War and the sound they made was compared to ripping lino. The gun entered service in 1942 and was considered of its time with its pressed steel body and relatively cheap cost. Another good feature of the gun was the fact that the barrel could be changed very quickly, unlike many Second World War machine guns. (*Author's Collection*)

Exhausted German troops rest behind a hedge during fighting in the spring of 1945 as they are pushed further northwards. It was surprising that the morale of the German Army in Italy held, despite all the reverses on the eastern and later north-west European fronts. *(Author's Collection)*

On 14 April 1944, Canadian Sherman M4 tanks cross the Sieve River, which flows into the Arno at Pontassieve, 10 miles to the east of Florence. They cross over a Bailey bridge, which was an example of the hardware that was arriving on the Italian Front by late 1944. Three Bailey bridges were built across the river overnight by the well-trained 8th Amy Engineers. More equipment arrived in Italy after the initial fighting in Normandy and was put to good use by the US and British forces. *(Author's Collection)*

An 8th Army mountain artillery unit sets up a firing position in the region of the Sillaro River in April 1945. The defences along the river, known as the Paula Line, were defended by the still fighting German 1st Paratroop Division. Ammunition for the US-supplied 75mm PACK howitzer has been brought forward by the mule train in the background of the photograph. (*Author's Collection*)

After taking a village in northern Italy in the spring of 1945, this New Zealander has turned an abandoned farmhouse into a temporary strongpoint with his Browning 0.5-inch M2 heavy machine gun. He probably belongs to the 4th New Zealand Armoured Brigade and has taken the machine from his Sherman tank to guard his comrades while they rest. There were two New Zealand units with the 8th Army in spring 1945 – the 2nd New Zealand Infantry Division and the Armoured Brigade. (*Author's Collection*)

Civilians are fleeing the fighting in northern Italy during the last months of the war and leave their town looking for refuge away from the front line. Their horse and cart passes a recently disabled Panzerkampfwagen V Panther, which had proven to be an excellent tank since its introduction in mid-1943. Although the Panther was a match for any Allied tank in 1945, there were simply not enough of them to counter the armour of the 8th and 5th armies. (*Author's Collection*)

British troops are moving towards the front line through German barbed wire obstacles during the battles for the Senio River in spring 1945. The Senio River was the last obstacle for the 8th Army in its advance into the Po Valley basin. When the Po Valley finally fell to the Allies, the war in northern Italy was effectively over. *(Author's Collection)*

A 3-inch mortar crew of the 'Jewish Infantry Brigade Group' is seen in action in spring 1945. Usually known as the Jewish Brigade, the 5,000-strong brigade had been raised in July 1944 from amongst the Jewish population of Palestine. It had three regiments (the 1st to the 3rd, and the 200th Artillery Regiment) and was sent to fight in northern Italy in October 1944. The Jewish Brigade took part in the battles along the Senio River, supported by the tanks of the North Irish Horse, in March 1945. *(Author's Collection)*

A British Army Churchill Mk IV A22 infantry tank moves towards Porto Maggiore, between Ferrara and Lake Comacchio, on 20 April, with infantry taking a ride into battle. The town was close to the Italian–Austrian border, and the 5th Battalion, the Northamptonshire Regiment, helped take it. When the war ended a few weeks later, they had just crossed the border into Austria as peace was declared. The Churchill, in service since 1940, was initially armed with a 2-pounder anti-tank, but the Mk IV had a 6-pounder main armament. It was a slow tank, with a maximum speed of 15 mph, compared to the Sherman M4, which had a speed of between 22 and 30 mph. (*Author's Collection*)

British troops clamber over a disabled Mk VI Tiger tank, which has been disabled by one of their comrades in fighting in northern Italy in April 1945. According to the original caption, the tank was put out of action by a soldier of the 8th Army using a PIAT anti-tank launcher. Although the Tiger was a well-armoured tank with an 88mm main armament, it was not indestructible. With the thickest frontal armour being 120mm, it would take a lucky shot on one of the more exposed points, which only had 25mm armour to disable it. (*Author's Collection*)

During the Spring Offensive through northern Italy, a US Army M10 tank destroyer moves through Querceta, a town along Highway 1. First brought into service in 1942, the M10 was a hybrid of a tank and a self-propelled gun with its rotating turret. It was the most important tank destroyer in Allied service, with some used by the British, Canadian and Free French forces. Although it was outclassed by the newer German Panther and Tiger tanks in Italy, it was still in widespread use until May 1945. (*US Army Archives*)

This medical team working on a wounded soldier belong to the 10th Medical Battalion of the US 10th Mountain Division. It had been raised as the 10th Light Division – 'Alpine' – in 1943, with the aim of having a specialist mountain formation to serve in Italy. In 1944, it was renamed as a Mountain unit and any specialist training it received was put to good use in the terrain of Italy. (*Author's Collection*)

A Sherman M4 tank moves through a northern Italian mountain village past a muleteer of the 10th Mountain Division in April 1945. The division was equipped with some specialist equipment, including snow ploughs and Weasel M29 tracked carriers. Its personnel were issued with white camouflage snowsuits and skis, which most them had been trained to use. (*US Army Archives*)

American soldiers of the 10th Mountain Division approach a village cautiously as even in April 1945, German units were holding out. Italy was covered in mountain villages and towns that could easily be turned into strongholds by the Germans. Most of the men in the platoon are armed with Garand M1 rifles but the man in the centre has a Browning M1919A4 light machine gun. (*US Army Archives*)

Three young female fighters belonging to the left-wing Partito D'Azione patrol the streets of Milan, which was liberated by Italian partisans on 25 April 1945. The well-armed 'amazons' are with some of their male comrades as they look for any hiding Fascists. These young women would have been babies when Mussolini came to power or may not even have been born when he rose to power in 1922. They would probably have been members of the various Fascist youth organisations in the 1930s, whose membership was more or less obligatory. (*Author's Collection*)

Italian partisans from the Po Valley take part in the Liberation of Bologna during April 1945 alongside the Polish II Corps. Partisans had captured large numbers of Italian arms during 1944 and were happy to assist the Allies in liberating their cities in northern Italy. After several weeks of heavy fighting, the city was finally fully liberated on 21 April. These men have acquired an M37 heavy machine gun from Italian stores and have set it up on one of the main streets of Bologna. (*US Army Archives*)

A recently delivered M24 Chafee light tank of the 81st Reconnaissance Squadron of the US 1st Armoured Division moves through the town of Vergato. The town was close to the city of Bologna, which was one of the main objectives of the Allied offensive of early 1945. Although lightly armoured, the Chafee was fast, with a top speed of 30 mph, and packed a punch for such a light vehicle with its 75mm M6 main gun. (*US Army Archives*)

Exhausted US soldiers have just entered the northern Italian city of Bologna on the morning of 21 April. One soldier has a nap in his jeep and rests his head on the steering wheel of his vehicle. While the US 5th Army advanced into the city from the south, Polish troops of the 8th Army came in from the east of Bologna. *(US Army Archives)*

Soldiers of the 88th Division move through a town in the Po Valley on 24 April looking for German snipers who are still active in the ruins. One of the 88th's regiments, the 349th, reached the Italian–Austrian border and joined up with the 103rd Division of the VI Corps of the 7th Army. The 103rd had advanced southwards through Bavaria and met up with the 349th at Vipiteno in the Italian Alps. *(US Army Archives)*

German prisoners stand calmly in a barbed wire enclosure guarded by a single American Military Policeman from US 4th Corps armed with a Garand M1 rifle. By the time the German Army in Italy had given up, they had lost most of their heavy weaponry and equipment. The morale of the average soldier had remained high until the final offensive, which pushed their resistance to the limit. The sheer weight of Allied firepower that they faced in spring 1945 finally broke their spirit. (*Author's Collection*)

Two German officers arrive at the headquarters of the British 6th Armoured Division on 7 May. They have come to negotiate a surrender with the commander of the division, whose tanks were held up on the road on the Italian–Austrian border by a series of German road blocks. (*Author's Collection*)

This crowd of German prisoners is gathered on the Po Plain having been chased down by the fast-moving Allied armoured columns in May 1945. By this stage in the campaign, the Germans had left their heavy weaponry and tanks behind and headed for the Austrian border. With no petrol available, German units had to rely on horses and carts to carry their equipment, as seen here. The wide-open terrain of the Po region was ideal for the tanks and armoured vehicles of the 5th and 8th armies, who surrounded and took the surrender of large German units. (*US Army Archives*)

In the last days of the war in Europe, there were meetings of some disparate allies like this one in Trieste on 2 May, between New Zealand troops and Yugoslavian partisans. The New Zealanders belong to the 2nd Division and have just fought their way for 30 miles to reach the Italian–Yugoslav border. By this time, the fighting in Italy had virtually ceased, although there were still some Germans fighting in the north of the country. (*Author's Collection*)

These Polish Cavalry belonging to the 10th Hussars and are pictured on parade at the end of the fighting in Italy in early May 1945. The regiment had a long tradition, and their insignia was added to the British Army battledress, with the Austrian knot on their berets. They also had a colour and pattern of button and cap badge that was unique to this unit. All three men seen here are armed with Thompson sub-machine guns, supplied to them via the USA. (*Polish Institute and Sikorski Museum Collection*)